UNDERSTANDING THE
HOLOCAUST

Nazi War Criminals

Don Nardo

ReferencePoint
Press®

San Diego, CA

About the Author

In addition to his many award-winning books on the ancient world, historian Don Nardo has written several studies of the ravages of World War II and the rise and fall of the Third Reich. Among them are an acclaimed biography of Adolf Hitler, overviews of Nazi Germany's rise and life in the Nazi concentration camps, and *Hitler in Paris*, an examination of the Nazi seizure of France and how Hitler used it as a propaganda tool. Nardo, who also composes and arranges orchestral music, lives with his wife, Christine, in Massachusetts.

© 2016 ReferencePoint Press, Inc.
Printed in the United States

For more information, contact:
ReferencePoint Press, Inc.
PO Box 27779
San Diego, CA 92198
www. ReferencePointPress.com

LIBRARY OF CONGRESS CATALOGING-IN-PUBLICATION DATA

Nardo, Don, 1947- author.
  Nazi war criminals / by Don Nardo.
    pages cm
  Includes bibliographical references and index.
  ISBN-13: 978-1-60152-850-6 (hardback)
  ISBN-10: 1-60152-850-7 (hardback)
  1. War criminals--Germany--Juvenile literature. 2. World War, 1939-1945--Atrocities--Juvenile literature. 3. Criminal investigation--Juvenile literature. I. Title.
  D804.34.N37 2016
  341.6'90268--dc23

                                                                    2015007518

CONTENTS

IMPORTANT EVENTS OF THE HOLOCAUST

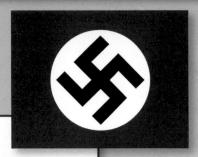

1941
Germany invades the Soviet Union; the Germans massacre about one hundred thousand Jews, Roma (Gypsies), Communists, and others at Babi Yar in Ukraine; the United States declares war on Japan and Germany after Japan attacks Pearl Harbor.

1937
Buchenwald concentration camp is established in east-central Germany.

1920
The Nazi Party publishes its 25-point program declaring its intention to segregate Jews from so-called Aryan society and to eliminate the political, legal, and civil rights of Germany's Jewish population.

1925
Adolf Hitler's autobiographical manifesto *Mein Kampf* is published; in it he outlines his political ideology and future plans for Germany and calls for the violent elimination of the world's Jews.

1940
The Warsaw ghetto—a 1.3 square mile (3.4 sq km) area sealed off from the rest of the city by high walls, barbed wire, and armed guards—is established in Poland.

1920 / 1934 1936 1938 1940

1918
The Treaty of Versailles, marking the formal end of World War I and a humiliating defeat for Germany, is signed.

1935
The Nuremberg Laws, excluding German Jews from citizenship and depriving them of the right to vote and hold public office, are enacted.

1939
Germany invades Poland, igniting World War II in Europe; in Warsaw, Jews are forced to wear white armbands with a blue Star of David.

1933
Hitler is appointed Germany's chancellor; the Gestapo is formed; Dachau concentration camp is established.

1938
Violent anti-Jewish attacks known as *Kristallnacht* (Night of Broken Glass) take place throughout greater Germany; the first *Kindertransport* (children's transport) arrives in Great Britain with thousands of Jewish children seeking refuge from Nazi persecution.

1942
The Nazi plan to annihilate Europe's Jews (the Final Solution) is outlined at the Wannsee Conference in Berlin; deportations of about 1.5 million Jews to killing centers in Poland begin.

1944
Allied forces carry out the D-Day invasion at Normandy in France; diplomats in Budapest offer protection to Jews.

1948
The State of Israel is established as a homeland for the world's Jews.

1946
The International Military Tribunal imposes death and prison sentences during the Nuremberg Trials.

1949
Argentina grants asylum to Josef Mengele, the notorious SS doctor who performed medical experiments on prisoners in Auschwitz.

1942   1944   1946   1948 / 1970

1943
Despite armed Jewish resistance, the Nazis move to liquidate ghettos in Poland and the Soviet Union; Denmark actively resists Nazi attempts to deport its Jewish citizens.

1960
In Argentina, Israeli intelligence agents abduct Adolf Eichmann, one of the masterminds of the Holocaust; he is brought to Israel to stand trial for crimes against the Jewish people.

1945
Allied forces liberate Auschwitz, Buchenwald, and Dachau concentration camps; Hitler commits suicide; World War II ends with the surrender of Germany and Japan; the Nuremberg Trials begin with war crimes indictments against leading Nazis.

1981
More than ten thousand survivors attend the first World Gathering of Jewish Holocaust Survivors in Israel; a similar gathering two years later in Washington, DC, attracts twenty thousand people.

1947
The UN General Assembly adopts a resolution partitioning Palestine into Jewish and Arab states; Holocaust survivor Simon Wiesenthal opens a center in Austria to search for Nazis who have evaded justice.

INTRODUCTION

Time Is Their Enemy

I n June 2013 residents of Minneapolis, Minnesota, were shocked to hear that a member of their community, ninety-four-year-old Michael Karkoc, had been accused of being a Nazi war criminal. A major US news organization, the Associated Press (AP), stated that it had uncovered the initial evidence for this charge. The AP further claimed that Karkoc had lied to US officials about his past. When he arrived in the United States from Ukraine in 1949, the AP report said, he told the officials that he had not served in the German military during World War II.

It was shortly before that largest, most destructive conflict in history that Adolf Hitler, head of Germany's Nazi Party, managed to seize control of that nation. After starting the war by invading Poland, Hitler and the Nazis set in motion an enormous and monstrous plan. Their hideous goal was to eradicate all Germans and other Europeans whom they viewed as inferior in one way or another. Their victims included Jews; Gypsies; Communists; Slavic peoples, including Russians and many Poles; disabled people; and gay people, among others.

The horrifying mass murders of members of these groups by the Nazis came to be called the Holocaust. At least 6 million Jews died in extermination camps in Germany, Poland, and elsewhere. Those same camps also witnessed the killings of the non-Jews the Nazis had targeted, bringing the Holocaust's overall death toll to at least 11 million and possibly as high as 17 million.

The Chlaniow Massacre

The nations that won the war, known as the Allies, labeled as war criminals the thousands of Nazis and others who had taken part in these crimes against humanity. According to the AP, Michael Karkoc was one of those wrongdoers. Supposedly, he commanded a Nazi SS-led unit that during the conflict burned Polish villages, killing hundreds of men, women, and children. (*SS* stands for *Schutzstaffel*, which translates to "Defense Corps" or "Protection Squadron." Hitler's main paramilitary group, it was involved in law enforcement and had charge of both Germany's secret police and several concentration camps.)

Supporting the AP's charges are statements made years earlier by members of Karkoc's unit. In 1967 one of Karkoc's soldiers, Vasyl Malazhenski, told Soviet authorities that in 1944 the unit was ordered to slaughter all the inhabitants of the Polish village of Chlaniow. "It was all like a trance," Malazhenski recalled, "setting the fires, the

German chancellor Adolf Hitler waves to the crowd during a parade. Hitler's invasion of Poland in September 1939 sparked World War II, the most destructive conflict in history.

shooting, the destroying. Later, when we were passing in file through the destroyed village, I could see the dead bodies of the killed residents: men, women, children."[1] Malazhenski and other members of the unit added that Karkoc was not only present at the massacre but also gave the command to commence the killing.

The AP report on Karkoc set off new investigations of him and his wartime unit. Reacting to these probes, in May 2014 Germany's highest criminal court, the Federal Court of Justice, ruled that it has the legal authority to try Karkoc. A few months later the Polish government made a similar ruling, based on the fact that most of the suspect's alleged crimes were against Poles on Polish territory. In February 2015 Karkoc was still awaiting prosecution, pending the collection of more evidence by US authorities.

> "I could see the dead bodies of the killed residents: men, women, children."[1]
>
> —SS guard Vasyl Malazhenski.

The Nazi Hunters

If the charges against Karkoc turn out to be true, it will mean that he, like many other Nazis, escaped Germany at the close of World War II. These fugitives managed to live in obscurity for decades, and some remain in hiding to this day.

Compared to most pursuits of alleged ex-Nazis, Karkoc's case was somewhat unusual. Whereas AP stumbled upon eyewitness testimony describing his wartime exploits, most Nazi war criminals are found by so-called Nazi hunters. One of the more visible of their number is Efraim Zuroff, director of the Jerusalem office of the Simon Wiesenthal Center. Founded in 1977 and headquartered in Los Angeles, California, its namesake was one of the most widely known survivors of the Nazi concentration camps. The center has seven offices around the globe, all dedicated to promoting human rights. The organization also devotes a hefty portion of its time and energies to tracking down escaped Nazi war criminals. Wiesenthal himself worked diligently at hunting such criminals right up to his death in 2005 at the age of ninety-six.

Among the other better-known Nazi hunting groups is the Israeli intelligence agency Mossad, established in 1951. Another is Germany's government-run Central Investigation Center for Nazi Crimes, presently under the direction of Kurt Schrimm. The United States has a similar group—the Justice Department's Office of Special Investigation, founded in 1979. In addition, a married couple—Serge and Beate Klarsfeld—has enjoyed considerable success bringing to justice hidden Nazi war criminals, including the infamous Butcher of Lyon, Klaus Barbie.

These and the other Nazi hunters know full well that their most formidable enemy is not any single former Nazi. Rather, that enemy is time. Most of the war criminals they seek are now in their nineties and rapidly dying off. "Someday there will be no more Nazi criminals to go after," Kurt Schrimm points out, "and then our organization will shut down." But until that day, he adds, "we will exhaust all investigation possibilities."[2]

CHAPTER ONE

The Coward's Way Out

By the early days of April 1945, it was clear that Nazi dictator Adolf Hitler's twisted dream of world conquest was over. Nazi Germany was in a state of utter collapse, as Hitler's enemies—the Allies—swiftly tightened the noose they had created around it. Their final target was the German capital, Berlin. There Hitler and his girlfriend, Eva Braun, awaited their inevitable end in an underground concrete bunker. On April 11, coming from the east, Soviet armies reached within 50 miles (80 km) of the city; coming from the west, meanwhile, American and British forces were some 62 miles (100 km) away and closing fast.

Hitler was not destined to stand trial for the countless murders and other atrocities he had perpetrated since he initiated the conflict in 1939. After marrying Braun in a brief ceremony in the bunker, on April 30 he helped her swallow toxic cyanide pills. Then he shot himself in the head.

A Growing List of War Criminals

Although Hitler had been the leading Nazi war criminal, he had not committed millions of murders all by himself. Hundreds of Nazi officers, including the commandants (senior officers) of concentration camps, had eagerly followed his ghastly orders. Repeatedly on their commands, hundreds and sometimes thousands of Jews, Slavs, Gypsies, and other peoples were herded together like cattle and cruelly killed each day.

Moreover, each of those ringleaders of the Holocaust had been aided by dozens and at times hundreds of his own officers, executioners, and other helpers. They had shot or gassed untold numbers of victims and either buried the bodies in mass graves or burned them in ovens. That gave these Nazi henchmen prominent places on Germany's growing list of war criminals.

During the conflict's final two years, these architects of mass slaughter were fully aware that their names were on that list. Indeed, it was clear to them that the Allies, who seemed increasingly likely to win the war, would arrest them and charge them as war criminals. The question was how those who operated the death camps would try to escape punishment. Some chose to destroy the evidence of their crimes by eliminating the gas chambers and other machinery of extermination. They figured they could simply deny having been involved in the genocide they had helped Hitler commit. (Genocide is the systematic destruction of an entire race or national group of people.) Others thought about fleeing in order to escape the justice the Allies were sure to impose on Hitler's Nazi disciples.

Engine of Death

In their desire to escape responsibility for their crimes, they recognized a serious obstacle. It was the great size and complexity of Germany's extermination operations and facilities. The problem was that the numerous physical aspects of those facilities could and would be used as evidence against them in any trials the Allies might hold after the war. In fact, well before Germany's collapse in early 1945, a number of leading Nazis worried about that potential damning evidence. As early as the second half of 1943, they began to order the dismantling of death camps that were no longer needed. All evidence of the mass killings that had occurred in them would, they hoped, be eliminated. That way, they reasoned, the camps' operators, along with higher-level Nazis, could deny that anything bad had happened in those places.

This is what took place at the Treblinka death camp, located a few miles northeast of Warsaw, in Poland. That Nazi facility was second only to Auschwitz (in southern Poland) in the number of prisoners it murdered during the war. Historians estimate that about 900,000 Jews and Gypsies died at Treblinka, compared to roughly 1.1 million Jews, Poles, Gypsies, and Soviet prisoners killed at Auschwitz.

The Treblinka death camp had opened in July 1942. Technically, it was called Treblinka II, to differentiate it from a nearby Nazi labor camp, Treblinka I. There, Polish civilians, some of them Jews, did backbreaking work in huge quarries and gravel pits. At Treblinka II,

Nearly 1 million people were murdered at the Nazi death camp located near the village of Treblinka, Poland.

meanwhile, the facilities for slaughtering human beings were perfected to the level of a well-organized machine. That engine of death operated almost twenty-four hours a day. A pamphlet distributed to modern tourists who visit the site's visitors' center sums up the awful carnage that occurred there. "The main part of the camp," it states,

> constituted two buildings in which there were 13 gas chambers altogether. Two thousand people could be put to death at a time in them. Death by suffocation with fumes came after 10 to 15 minutes. First the bodies of the victims were buried, later were cremated on big grates out of doors. The ashes were mixed with sand and buried in one spot.

> Killing took place with great speed. The whole process of killing the people, starting from their arrival at the camp railroad,

till removing the corpses from the gas chambers, lasted about 2 hours. Treblinka was known among the Nazis as an example of good organization of a death camp. It was a real extermination centre.[3]

Choosing the Second Option

By August 1943 almost all the Jews and other so-called inferiors who had lived in northern Poland had been eliminated in Treblinka's death camp. Therefore high Nazi authorities considered the facility's work to be finished. At that point, it had two possible fates. One was to remain in place in case the Nazis might need it again in the future, perhaps to exterminate the millions of Soviets whom Hitler planned to eradicate eventually. Or the camp could be torn down in order to get rid of any evidence of the part it had played in the Holocaust.

The Nazis, including the camp's three successive commandants, chose the second option, likely out of guilt and fear that they might someday be called to task for their crimes. By October 1943 much of Treblinka II was gone. (The Treblinka labor camp continued operating well into 1944.) The gas chambers and large outdoor stone grates, on which most of the bodies had been burned, were covered with dirt. In a ghoulish touch, the prisoners who did most of this work were ordered to plant flowers in that tainted soil. Afterward, those inmates were taken to another death camp and speedily executed.

> "Treblinka was known among the Nazis as an example of good organization of a death camp. It was a real extermination centre."[3]
>
> —Treblinka visitors' center informational pamphlet.

With Treblinka II no longer in operation, its last commandant, Kurt Franz, was transferred to a post in northern Italy. There, in the last two months of 1943, he was reunited with a man he had worked with before—Treblinka II's prior commandant, Franz Stangl. Both men were glad that the death camp they had operated had been eliminated. For Stangl, it was partly a matter of bad memories, since he was sick of the sight and smell of death. He later recalled "the pits full of blue-black corpses." That most of these bodies belonged to human beings who died under his watch did not bother him particularly. "It had nothing to do with humanity," he admitted. "It couldn't have," because "it was a mass—a mass of rotting flesh."[4]

Stangl had another reason to be glad that the Treblinka death camp had been dismantled. Shortly before Franz's arrival in northern Italy, in September 1943 the Americans, aided by other Allies, had assaulted German-held Italy. In less than a month they had captured the entire southern half of the country and now pressed northward with renewed vigor. If they managed to make it into Poland, Stangl felt, it would be best if they found no evidence that the camp had been used for mass killings.

> "It had nothing to do with humanity. It couldn't have [because] it was a mass—a mass of rotting flesh."[4]
>
> —Treblinka commandant Franz Stangl.

Stangl, Franz, and other death camp commandants found even more to concern them in late 1943 and early 1944. Not only were the Allies on a solid winning streak, but also disturbing reports had been filtering through the rumor mill within the ranks of Nazi officers. Some of the buzz claimed that Hitler was incompetent. Other rumors said that he was a madman who might be leading Germany to ultimate ruin. These and other factors made Germany's eventual defeat seem possible, if not quite probable.

The Angel of Death

While the death camp leaders worried about their possible fates, some of their more notorious Nazi colleagues felt they had even more to lose. One of them was the man commonly known as the "Angel of Death," Dr. Josef Mengele. He had joined the SS in 1938, coincidentally the same year he obtained his medical degree. While serving on the eastern front, Mengele was badly wounded. After recovering, he received a promotion to the rank of captain and in May 1943 was appointed to work as a doctor at the infamous Auschwitz death camp.

There, in addition to his regular medical duties, including caring for sick guards and other staff, Mengele spent a great deal of time pursuing bizarre medical research. Over time these activities earned him a widespread reputation for sickening cruelty, sadism, and inhumanity. In fact, he treated prisoners so mercilessly that even some of the camp's battle-hardened SS officers feared him.

Prisoners arrive at the Auschwitz concentration camp. As soon as the prisoners arrived, Nazi guards inspected them, deciding on the spot who would live and who would die.

One of Mengele's jobs was to inspect the trainloads of incoming prisoners and decide which of them would be gassed and burned and which would participate in his gruesome medical experiments. Most of these researches were built around his extreme fascination for genetics, the study of genes and heredity. In one repeated experiment, he castrated male prisoners without giving them painkillers. He also dissected live babies, who also received no anesthetics, and injected colored dyes into children's eyes to determine if their eye color would permanently change. The victims who received the dyes frequently went blind. Some actually died, after which Mengele cut out their eyes and pinned them to a wall in his office.

The Husband and Wife Nazi Hunters

Among the best-known European Nazi hunters are husband and wife Serge and Beate Klarsfeld. Serge is a French Jew who still remembers narrowly escaping arrest by Hitler's secret police, the Gestapo, when he was a child. Later his father died in the infamous death camp known as Auschwitz. Beate, meanwhile, was born in Germany in 1939 and as a child did not realize the extent of the awful atrocities committed by her country during the war. It was when she moved to Paris in 1960 and met Serge that she finally learned about the details of the Holocaust and developed a strong sense of moral outrage at what Nazi Germany had done in the early 1940s.

Another source of moral outrage for both Serge and Beate was the realization that many former Nazis had not been found and punished for their war crimes. One was Kurt Kiesinger, who was elected chancellor of Germany in 1966. The Klarsfelds put together a detailed report on Kiesinger's wartime activities and gave it to the press, which in part led to his defeat in the next election for chancellor. Thereafter, the Klarsfelds devoted themselves to finding and exposing other former Nazis who had been evading arrest and prosecution.

Their most famous catch was Klaus Barbie, whose wartime brutality as a Gestapo officer in France had earned him the nickname the "Butcher of Lyon." Thanks to their efforts, in the early 1980s he was arrested, tried, and imprisoned for life.

The Angel of Death believed that the people he experimented on would not be missed. He considered them to be inferior human specimens, members of the "idiot masses" who were dragging down the human race. In his diary he wrote, "Everything will end in catastrophe if natural selection is altered to the point that gifted people are overwhelmed by billions of morons. We have to prevent the rise of the idiot masses. Inferior morons should be exterminated."[5]

The Auschwitz Death March

By the end of 1944, it was clear to the Nazis working at Auschwitz that the onrushing Soviets would reach them within mere weeks. Mengele knew that his name must be high on the Allied list of war criminals that were to be captured, tried, and possibly executed. So he prepared to flee.

At that moment, the death camp was in an uproar. Everyone realized that there was not enough time to dismantle the gas chambers and other major incriminating evidence, as had been done at Treblinka and some other camps. They *could* remove the human evidence, however. So SS men rounded up some sixty thousand prisoners and got ready to lead them out of the camp. The commandant, officers, and guards, along with Mengele and his small medical staff, gathered all the belongings they could carry, and on January 17, 1945, the strategic retreat began.

Those in charge hoped to take the prisoners overland to another camp, where they would be put to work or temporarily warehoused. Most of the march-

> "We have to prevent the rise of the idiot masses. Inferior morons should be exterminated."[5]
>
> —Nazi physician Josef Mengele.

ers were already frail, weak, and half-starved, and it only got worse for them. Their captors heartlessly drove them on, mile after mile in snow and freezing temperatures, denying them food, water, or rest. Many fell along the way. The guards abruptly shot these unfortunate stragglers.

At the conclusion of the death march, Mengele and some of his associates continued to flee westward. At that point he was unaware that Soviet troops had arrived in the Auschwitz death camp on January 27, ten days after its staff had escaped. Moreover, like other Nazi war criminals now on the run, Mengele had no assurances that he would survive the huge outburst of chaos and death that was then enveloping Germany. Nor did he have any idea where he would go if he *did* escape both the turmoil and capture.

The Butcher of Riga

At that moment, many miles away, Stangl and Franz found themselves in the same predicament. Stangl had recently left northern Italy, which the Allies had finally overrun, and he hoped to find his wife and make a run for it. An Allied unit soon captured him. But its leaders did not realize who he was, and he managed to escape and keep running. Meanwhile, Franz got rid of his SS uniform and changed his name in hopes of melting back into the civilian German population.

Another Nazi of similar rank to Stangl and Franz—Eduard Roschmann—also found himself on the run as the Allies poured into Germany. Roschmann, an Austrian by birth, had joined the Nazi Party and then the SS in the 1930s. In 1941 he was assigned to work for the director of secret police in Riga, the capital of Latvia (located north-east of Poland and Germany), which the Nazis had recently seized.

Visitors place flowers at the site of a destroyed synagogue in Riga, Latvia. Many of Riga's Jews were tortured and murdered by Nazi Eduard Roschmann, known as the "Butcher of Riga."

Swiftly rising through the ranks, Roschmann became commandant of Riga's Jewish ghetto, the run-down section of town in which Jews were forced to live. As was the case with most ghetto commandants across Nazi-held Europe, he was given a free hand, which he proceeded to use like an iron fist. Historians estimate that he tortured and killed numerous Jews with his own hands and overall was responsible for the deaths of some eighty thousand Jews. These heinous acts earned him the nickname the "Butcher of Riga."

In October 1944 the Soviets were rapidly advancing on Riga, and the Germans in Latvia were in a hasty retreat. Among them were Roschmann and his staff of SS thugs. Desperate to escape, they hurried to the docks along the bay leading to the Baltic Sea. There they saw that some wounded German soldiers were boarding a small ship that would take them to safety. Roschmann approached the soldiers' captain and demanded that he empty the vessel and hand it over to the SS. When the captain refused, Roschmann drew his pistol and without hesitation shot and killed him. In the ruckus that ensued, the SS men fled, leaving their commandant to fend for himself. He managed to escape Latvia by wearing a corporal's uniform and blending into the crowds of German troops heading back toward Germany.

Roschmann was soon arrested by the Americans, but he escaped once again. Later the British also arrested him, and this time he escaped by jumping from a moving train that was carrying German prisoners of war. Free once more, Roschmann joined the ranks of Nazi war criminals who were frantically seeking a way to evade capture.

Steward of the Final Solution

Among those tattered ranks was Adolf Eichmann. Next to Hitler, he was one of the highest-placed Nazi war criminals, with the blood of millions on his hands. Eichmann joined the Nazi Party and SS in 1932. Like Roschmann, he rose quickly through the SS ranks. By October 1939 Eichmann was in charge of the Central Office for Jewish Emigration, tasked with finding ways of ridding Germany of Jews.

At first Eichmann and other Nazi leaders considered forcing Jews to leave the country. But as the war progressed, Hitler made the decision to employ the so-called Final Solution—the mass murder of all Jews in Europe. At that point, Eichmann, widely seen as the Nazis'

"They Were Cargo"

Many of the Nazi SS officers who ran Hitler's extermination camps, including Franz Stangl, a commandant at Treblinka, expressed few or no moral regrets for what they had done during the war. In Stangl's mind, for instance, the Jews, Gypsies, and others he had killed were more objects than people. So their eradication was not murder in the usual sense. This twisted conception stood out in an interview Stangl gave Austrian journalist Gitta Sereny in 1970. At one point Sereny asked him if he ever got used to the mass killings.

Stangl: "I made myself concentrate on work, work and again work."

Sereny: "Would it be true to say that you finally felt they weren't really human beings?"

Stangl: "When I was on a trip once, years later in Brazil, my train stopped next to a slaughterhouse. The cattle in the pens, hearing the noise of the train, trotted up to the fence and stared at the train. They were very close to my window, one crowding the other, looking at me through that fence. I thought then, 'Look at this, this reminds me of Poland; that's just how the people [I sent to the gas chambers] looked. . . . Those big eyes which looked at me not knowing that in no time at all they'd all be dead."

Sereny: "So you didn't feel they were human beings?"

Stangl: "Cargo. They were cargo."

Quoted in the Holocaust Website, "Sobibor: Franz Stangl." www.auschwitz.dk.

"Jewish expert," seemed the natural choice to lead the operation. He eagerly took charge of shipping Jews from the ghettos in which they had been compelled to reside to Treblinka, Auschwitz, and the other extermination camps.

In the conflict's final months, Eichmann was not exactly sure how many Jews he had sent to certain death. But he knew it was at least 5 million, as revealed in a remark he made to one of his henchmen. The topic of Germany's imminent defeat came up, along with the possibility that Eichmann might be captured and executed. The steward of the Final Solution responded to that notion by smiling. Then he remarked that he would "leap laughing into the grave because the feeling that I had five million people on my conscience would be for me a source of extraordinary satisfaction."[6]

This show of fearlessness was soon proved bogus by Eichmann's extreme desire to save his skin. Instead of standing up and defending his beliefs and actions like other top-ranking Nazis, he chose the coward's way out. He tossed away his SS uniform and forged some ID papers that listed his name as Otto Eckmann. These helped him when the Americans captured him in early 1945 because at first they did not realize who he really was. This gave him time to escape, and once more he was on the run, along with Stangl, Franz, Roschmann, and numerous others. In the years to come, many of them would be variously hunted down, captured, tried, and sentenced to pay for their unspeakable war crimes.

> "The feeling that I had five million people on my conscience would be for me a source of extraordinary satisfaction."[6]
>
> —Adolf Eichmann, one of the architects of Hitler's Final Solution.

CHAPTER TWO

Former Nazis on the Run

World War II in Europe ended in early May 1945. On May 2 German forces in Berlin surrendered to the Allies, and between the third and eighth of that month German armies in other parts of Germany and Europe did the same. One of the most important goals set by Allied leaders in the weeks that followed was to round up as many of the principal Nazis as possible. Millions of people had lost their lives at the hands of Hitler and his chief followers. It was therefore seen as imperative that those men be tried and punished for their crimes against humanity.

Hitler had taken his own life a few days before his nation's surrender, thus escaping any possibility of retribution. Two of his major accomplices had done the same. On May 1, 1945, the day before Berlin's surrender, Joseph Goebbels, the Nazi propaganda minister, and his wife, Magda, were in Hitler's bunker beneath the city. The couple killed their six sleeping children by slipping cyanide pills into their mouths, then killed themselves (although exactly how they took their own lives is uncertain). Heinrich Himmler, the chief Nazi administrator, was caught by Allied soldiers on May 21 and swallowed a cyanide pill two days later that he had hidden on his person.

Of the many leading Nazis who survived, some were captured in the initial days following the war's end and jailed awaiting their inevitable trials for war crimes. Among others, they included the Nazi Party's secretary, Martin Bormann; the longest serving commandant of the infamous Auschwitz death camp, Rudolf Hoess; and the original head of the Gestapo (secret police), Hermann Göring.

Germany's New President

A number of other foremost Nazis managed to remain free longer. At the close of the conflict, for example, Kurt Franz, the last commandant at the Treblinka death camp, blended back into the shell-shocked, disorganized German population. After changing his name, he worked for a while as a laborer on bridge projects and then became a cook. He was not caught and jailed until 1959.

A few other leading Nazis did not even attempt to run or hide. The most prominent of their number was Karl Dönitz, who served as commander of Nazi Germany's navy during most of the war. Shortly before Hitler killed himself, he appointed Dönitz the new president of Germany.

As a longtime patriotic military officer, Dönitz chose to do his duty rather than to run away as the Allies seized control of his country. During his three weeks as president, he ordered several German generals to surrender and went through the motions of running the nation. There was "no possibility of affecting any improvement in Germany's overall position by political means," he later recalled. So, "the only conclusion to which I, as head of state, could come was that the war must be brought to an end as quickly as possible in order to prevent further bloodshed."[7] Dönitz peacefully awaited the Allies' arrival and handed over his office to them on May 23, 1945.

> "The war must be brought to an end as quickly as possible in order to prevent further bloodshed."[7]
>
> —President of Nazi Germany Karl Dönitz.

The Beast of Belsen

Another important Nazi who gave himself up to the Allies without a fuss was Josef Kramer, who worked at several Nazi concentration camps during the war. Among his many war crimes, Kramer was especially infamous for helping some leading Nazis collect Jewish skeletons for research. To fulfill that vile order, he personally gassed eighty Jews to death at the Natzweiler-Struthof concentration camp in France.

Later, Kramer became second in charge at Auschwitz. Then, near the end of 1944, he was appointed to the post of commandant at the Bergen-Belsen concentration camp in northern Germany. During the short time he ran that facility, he gained a reputation for cruelty that inspired the prisoners' nickname for him—the "Beast of Belsen."

Josef Kramer (center) was the Nazi commandant at the Bergen-Belsen concentration camp. When British troops arrived to liberate the camp, Kramer gave them a tour of the facility that revealed more than thirteen thousand unburied corpses.

In the beginning of 1945, a terrible outbreak of typhus erupted in the Bergen-Belsen camp. As many as three hundred prisoners died from the disease each day. In April, with Nazi Germany in collapse, most of the camp's guards and medical personnel fled, but Kramer and a few of his staff members stayed behind. When a unit of British troops arrived to liberate the camp, Kramer surprised the officers by offering to take them on a tour of the facility. They were revolted by the piles of unburied bodies, amounting to more than thirteen thousand in all. One British officer later said that some of the surviving prisoners "were so weak that when we went in there we had a job to tell the living from the dead. Skeletons, they were." Most were covered with lice and suffering from typhus. He added, "the smell was the worst. You couldn't get it out of your nostrils for days."[8]

Some of the Allied officers, including a British doctor, later remarked that Kramer seemed unmoved by the horrific scene. It was almost as if he was proud to show off his work, they said. The doctor described Kramer as "a typical German brute—a sadistic, heavy-featured Nazi. He was quite unashamed."[9]

A Forged Passport

An unknown number of the Nazi officers and guards who had helped engineer the Holocaust decided their best bet was to flee Germany. Some made it out of the country and went into hiding in neighboring lands. But quite a few others ran much farther—across the oceans to other continents, particularly South America.

Franz Stangl, the former commandant of Treblinka, was one of those long-range escapees. At war's end he found himself back in Italy. There he talked to some other Nazis on the run who told him about an unusual opportunity. Several cardinals (high-ranking members of the Roman Catholic clergy) from the Vatican in Rome had set up a secret network to help escaped Nazis reach safe havens outside of Europe. In 1948 those churchmen gave Stangl forged Red Cross travel documents that got him to Syria, on the eastern Mediterranean coast just south of Turkey. Soon Stangl's wife and children joined him there. In 1951 the family moved to Brazil. There, aided by other former Nazis, Stangl found a job at the Volkswagen plant in São Paulo, on that nation's southern coast. Incredibly, he used his real name and for many years felt little or no fear of being caught.

Today some people find it strange that a known Nazi war criminal could escape arrest in Brazil or anywhere else for so long. Part

> "The smell was the worst. You couldn't get it out of your nostrils for days."[8]
>
> —A British officer who took part in the liberation of the Bergen-Belsen death camp.

of the problem was that German authorities were busy for years cleaning up and rebuilding the country and guarding war criminals that were already in German jails. So no arrest warrant was issued against Stangl until 1961. Also, even *with* a warrant, the authorities were unsure of exactly where he was in Brazil. As it turned out,

The Jewish Skeleton Collection

The Natzweiler-Struthof concentration camp in which Josef Kramer gassed eighty-six Jews to collect their skeletons was located atop a small mountain in northeastern France. The facility was not originally built to do large-scale executions of Jews and the other peoples Hitler deemed undesirable. Rather, the camp was mainly used to jail German criminals and French resistance fighters.

Early in the war, however, SS chief Heinrich Himmler approved a project submitted to him by an SS captain named August Hirt. It called for killing dozens of Jews in order to harvest their skeletons for a study. Supposedly, it would show that Jews were physically inferior to other people. For various reasons, the decision was made to carry out the executions at the Natzweiler-Struthof camp. Kramer was then the commandant of the facility, so the grisly job fell to him.

Of the eighty-six victims, twenty-nine were women and fifty-seven were men. They were murdered in a makeshift gas chamber in the first week following their arrival at the camp in August 1943. Today a museum exists at Natzweiler-Struthof, and one of the key items displayed is Kramer's confession to killing eighty of the subjects himself. In that document, he tells how he created the poison gas by combining certain deadly substances with water. He then drilled a hole in the wall of the death chamber (normally used to refrigerate food) and inserted the gas through it. Kramer watched the victims' death agonies through a second hole he had made in the wall.

the noted Nazi hunter Simon Wiesenthal found Stangl's location in 1967, at which time German agents finally arrested the former Treblinka commandant.

The Butcher's Luck Runs Out

Another Nazi war criminal who ended up in South America was Eduard Roschmann, the so-called Butcher of Riga. After jumping from a moving train to escape custody of the Allies in 1948, he slipped quietly into Italy. There, with the aid of a Catholic bishop, he managed to get phony identification papers that allowed him to go to the South American country of Argentina. He settled near the country's capital, Buenos Aires, and worked as a travel agent.

In 1955 Roschmann made a serious blunder. Although still married to his wife, who had remained in Germany when he fled, he got married again, this time to his secretary. Within a few months, his German wife found out about the second, illegal marriage, and to get revenge for this betrayal, she reported him to the German authorities. This forced him to begin moving frequently from place to place within Argentina, counting on the existing network of local fellow Nazis to help him. Roschmann remained on the run for almost two decades. But his streak of good luck eventually changed. In 1972 novelist Frederick Forsyth published *The Odessa File*, a book in which Roschmann was the main character. Though partially fictional, the book does contain numerous true depictions of its subject's wartime activities and escape from Latvia, including his cold-blooded murder of a German officer on the docks at Riga.

Two years later a Hollywood movie version of the novel was released. Not long after the film began playing in Argentina, Roschmann found to his dismay that he no longer had the support of most of the former Nazis there. They had not known about his killing of a fellow German to make good his escape, and now they no longer trusted him. That made it much more difficult for him to find lodgings that were safe from the prying eyes of Nazi hunters. As a result, in 1977 one of their number—Wiesenthal—discovered where Roschmann was living. Then, in a twist worthy of a sequel

This scene is from the movie The Odessa File, *which is based on a fictionalized account of Nazi Eduard Roschmann's wartime activities and later escape to Argentina.*

to *The Odessa File*, as the authorities closed in on the former Nazi, he suffered a heart attack and died. The Butcher of Riga's luck had finally run out.

Hunting for the Most Wanted

Two of the most-wanted former Nazis—Josef Mengele and Adolf Eichmann—also ended up in or near Buenos Aires. After arriving there in 1949, Mengele, the doctor that had performed gruesome experiments on prisoners in Auschwitz, initially worked as a carpenter and later sold farm equipment. For the latter job, he started taking sales trips to nearby Paraguay in 1951. Some evidence suggests that he also practiced medicine without a license for a while and in that capacity performed abortions. More certain is that he obtained Paraguayan citizenship in 1959.

That same year, some Nazi hunters found Mengele's home address in Buenos Aires and urged the German government to issue an arrest warrant. Realizing that he might be captured, he fled to Paraguay and eventually to Brazil. There he bought a half-interest in a cattle farm and continued to live comfortably. Mengele's relatively easy life came to sudden end in 1979 when he suffered a stroke while swimming and drowned.

Meanwhile, Adolf Eichmann arrived in Buenos Aires in 1948, thanks to his acquisition of fake Red Cross travel documents from an Austrian Catholic bishop. Once settled in Argentina, the architect of Hitler's continent-wide mass murders managed to find a good job at the local Mercedes-Benz plant. In the years that followed, Wiesenthal and other Nazi hunters searched diligently for him.

Eventually, the Israeli government also became involved in the operation. Agents of Mossad tracked down and captured Eichmann in May 1960. Then the Israelis gave him a very public trial that was viewed on television throughout the world and executed him in May 1962. His last words were: "Long live Germany. Long live Argentina. Long live Austria. These are the three countries with which I have been most connected and which I will not forget. I greet my wife, my family and my friends. I am ready. We'll meet again soon, as is the fate of all men. I die believing in God."[10] The Israelis cremated the body at a secret site and scattered the ashes in the Mediterranean Sea.

Travel Along the Rat Lines

Even a brief examination of the cases of Roschmann, Mengele, and Eichmann reveals a definite pattern in their escape methods and destinations. First, a great many former Nazis got out of Europe using phony documents that identified them as Red Cross workers.

Possibly as many as eight hundred escapees reached Argentina alone in this way.

Second, those escape routes, which came to be called "rat lines," were often set up by cardinals, bishops, and other Vatican agents. Led by Bishop Alois Hudal, these right-wing churchmen distrusted or hated Jews and thought that democracy caters to society's lowest elements. So that group of leading European Catholics embraced the anti-Semitism (hatred of Jews) and strong-arm tactics of Hitler and other right-wing dictators.

In some cases, however, European churchmen were unable to help the war criminals get the proper papers to travel. So powerful individuals working inside South American governments secretly supplied such documents, usually for a price. For example, the corrupt Argentine president Juan Perón sold an estimated ten thousand passports to Germans and other Europeans fleeing Europe in the last months of World War II.

The third and perhaps most important part of the pattern established by Roschmann and others was the fact that a majority of the rat lines led to South America. Historians and other experts estimate that as many as nine thousand Nazi war criminals successfully entered that continent in the first few years following the war. It appears that Argentina took in more of these refugees—some five thousand—than any other South American nation. Somewhere between fifteen hundred and two thousand ended up in Brazil; from five hundred to one thousand in Chile; and smaller numbers in Paraguay and Uruguay.

One reason why these countries were willing to take in former Nazis was political in nature. In the immediate postwar years, several South American nations were governed by fascist (extreme right-wing) dictators who agreed with many of the vile policies Hitler and his Nazis had implemented. Another reason those countries welcomed former Nazis was economic in nature. Many of the refugees had considerable experience in business, government administration, military matters, or scientific research. It was thought that such talents might help local companies thrive and thereby expand the various South American economies. German scientists were seen

How Dr. Death Evaded Capture

One of the more unusual cases of former Nazis on the run following World War II was that of Dr. Aribert Heim, widely known as "Dr. Death." He earned this name for his commission of gruesome war crimes while serving as a doctor at the Mauthausen concentration camp. Witnesses said that he performed experimental operations on inmates, including the injection of various substances into people's hearts to determine which ones killed them the fastest.

At the close of the war, some American soldiers captured Heim. But at the time they knew nothing of his heinous war crimes, so they released him.

For a few years he worked as a physician in the German town of Baden-Baden. But in 1962 he heard that an arrest warrant had at last been issued for him, so he escaped. Knowing that many Nazis had gone to South America, Heim decided to try to throw authorities off his trail by going to Egypt. There he successfully hid for many years using the phony name Tarek Hussein Farid. To avert suspicion of who he really was, he even went so far as to convert to Islam. The Simon Wiesenthal Center eventually listed him as the most wanted Nazi war criminal and offered a reward of $405,000 for any information leading to his arrest. Heim was never captured, however, and died in Egypt of cancer in 1992.

as particularly valuable. This explains why, between 1945 and 1950 alone, about sixty German scientists moved to Argentina and were immediately given positions working in their professions.

Distrust Among the Allies

Not all former Nazis and their close supporters ended up in South America. At least a few hundred of them escaped from Europe and

Despite his membership in the Nazi Party, Wernher von Braun (pictured), like many other scientists, was allowed to settle in the United States. There, von Braun worked on the American space program.

found safety with right-wing governments in the Middle East. Even some of the Allies secretly helped some former Nazis escape capture. In these unusual cases, the expertise of German scientists was again the main attraction.

On the one hand, the Soviet Union, Britain, and United States all wanted to benefit from the knowledge of these experts. On the other, the US and Soviet governments did not trust each other and knew that a so-called cold war was developing between the two nations. So each sought to keep former German scientists out of the other's hands. As a result, more than fifteen hundred physicists, chemists, engineers, technicians, and other experts from Nazi Germany were quietly resettled in the United States. Among them were Wernher von Braun and other rocket scientists who would later form the core of the US space agency, NASA.

Thus, some of individuals who left Germany after the war were scientists who worked on weapons for Germany's war effort. Others, like Stangl and Roschmann, were SS or Gestapo officers who regularly ordered the killings of untold numbers of people. No matter which group of escapees they were in, all of them made sure to keep abreast of the daily or weekly news beginning in November 1945. In the months to come, most of the world's attention would be riveted on the German city of Nuremberg, where the top Nazi leaders already in custody were tried for crimes against humanity.

CHAPTER THREE

The Nuremberg Trials

After the Allies defeated Nazi Germany in early 1945, the enormous war effort against that nation was finally over. But it immediately became clear to the leaders of the victorious countries that a new and no less important effort was needed. Namely, the chief Nazis, who had ordered the commission of numerous appalling crimes against humanity, had to be tried and punished.

Hitler, the main engineer of the Nazi horrors, could not be punished, because he was dead. Likewise, his trusted henchmen, SS commander Heinrich Himmler and Nazi propaganda minister Joseph Goebbels, had taken their own lives. Moreover, a few of the leading Nazis, including Adolf Eichmann, had managed to escape.

Yet several of those top Nazis were alive and in custody, and it was they who became the focus of the first round of war crimes trials. These proceedings took place in the city of Nuremberg, in south-central Germany, so they fittingly became known as the Nuremberg Trials. In all, twenty-one defendants, all men, were tried and sentenced. (The initial number of accused was twenty-three. However, one of them, Martin Bormann, could not be located, and another, Robert Ley, committed suicide during the trials.) Among the twenty-one were Nazi Party leader Rudolf Hess; Gestapo boss and air force chief Hermann Göring; navy admiral and Germany's president (for three weeks) Karl Dönitz; governor of Nazi-held Poland Hans Frank; army leader Wilhelm Keitel; armaments minister and Hitler's personal architect Albert Speer; and Nazi Party philosopher Alfred Rosenberg.

In the weeks following the start of the trials in November 1945, many observers, both inside and outside the courtroom, registered genuine surprise. Glancing at the accused men sitting together on one side of the room, they had expected to see a bunch of ugly, snarling monsters whose looks matched the heinous crimes they had committed. Instead, they beheld several rather ordinary-looking men who could have passed as the father, uncle, or grandfather in a typical German family.

Indeed, that these average-appearing individuals were responsible for such unspeakable crimes seemed weirdly perplexing and disconcerting to many people at the time. Later the great German-born American thinker Hannah Arendt summed up this disturbing reality using the word *banality*, meaning ordinariness or normalcy. Referring to the leading Nazis, she famously wrote, "This long course in human wickedness had taught us the lesson of the fearsome, word-and-thought-denying banality of evil."[11] That is, often the worst crimes are committed by unassuming, seemingly normal people. Therefore, there is no certain way to predict who will end up inflicting cruelty and brutality on others.

Prosecutors and Judges

Regardless of how the defendants looked or seemed, they had undoubtedly committed terrible crimes. Most of the more than 50 million deaths in World War II—a number that included soldiers, civilians, and Holocaust victims—had occurred in Europe as a result of actions initiated by Nazi Germany's leaders. With this in mind, the Allies planned to openly broadcast the trials to the world to make an example of the Nazi war criminals. They hoped this would deter such brutality and mass murder in the future.

US president Harry Truman chose Supreme Court justice Robert Jackson to act as the chief prosecutor for the United States at the trials. In June 1945 Jackson traveled to London to meet with prosecutors and other officials from the other Allied powers—France, Britain, and the Soviet Union. Over time they set the ground rules for the upcoming legal proceeding in Nuremberg. They decided to call it the International Military Tribunal and to use one primary and one alternate judge from each of the four main Allies.

The four primary judges first met in Nuremberg on October 13, 1945. Representing the United States on the bench was Francis Biddle, who, like Jackson, was appointed by Truman. Also, the Allies agreed that Britain's primary judge, Sir Geoffrey Lawrence, should be the court's presiding, or head, judge.

Meanwhile, in the weeks leading up to the opening of the tribunal, the staffs for each of the chief prosecutors arrived to set up shop. Jackson's staff alone included more than six hundred lawyers, legal

Major European War Crimes Trials, 1943–1947

Although top Nazi leaders were tried for war crimes in the city of Nuremberg, Germany, similar trials of lower-ranking party members were held in cities all over Europe.

Oslo
NORWAY
North Sea
SWEDEN
IRELAND
DENMARK
Copenhagen
SOVIET UNION
GREAT BRITAIN
Hamburg
Bialystok
Lüneburg
POLAND
The Hague
Brunswick
Poznan
Warsaw
NETHERLANDS
Wuppertal Leipzig
Lodz
BELGIUM
GERMANY
Auschwitz Krakow
Lublin
Kiev
Kharkov
LUX. (Occupied)
Paris
Prague
FRANCE
Nuremberg
CZECHOSLOVAKIA
Dachau
Vienna
Bratislava
SWITZ. AUSTRIA
Budapest
Krasnodar
(Occupied)
HUNGARY
ITALY
Ljubljana
ROMANIA
Zagreb
Bucharest
Belgrade
Black Sea
SPAIN
Rome
YUGOSLAVIA
BULGARIA
TURKEY
ALBANIA
1945 International borders
GREECE

• Solid dots represent select sites of war crimes trials.

aides, and secretaries. One reason so many individuals were needed was the sheer volume of the evidence to sort through and consider. The captured Nazi documents that contained the proof of the prisoners' crimes numbered more than one hundred thousand.

The World Bathed in Blood

As the tribunal began its work on November 20, 1945, the accused war criminals entered the courtroom and sat in the dock (a raised platform lined with chairs), which faced the bench where the judges sat. The defendants were guarded by six well-armed American soldiers. Next the four primary judges walked in and sat in their seats behind the bench. In a sober, straightforward manner, Lawrence called the proceedings to order, after which the indictments, or charges against the defendants, were read aloud.

The first charge was "conspiracy to wage aggressive war," and the second was the commission of "crimes against peace." The third indictment cited the commission of "war crimes," defined as the abuse or murder of prisoners of war and employment of weapons and devices banned by international law. This included poison gas and the chambers in which it had been used. The last charge, "crimes against humanity,"[12] included the persecution and systematic (organized) slaughter of Jews, Gypsies, and other ethnic minorities, disabled people, and other groups. The list of specific crimes against humanity was so long that simply reading it took the entire first day.

The following day, the main American prosecutor, Jackson, gave the opening statement for the prosecution. "These prisoners represent sinister influences that will lurk in the world long after their bodies have returned to dust," he began. "We will show them to be living symbols of racial hatreds, of terrorism and violence, and of the arrogance and cruelty of power."[13] After spending nearly two hours describing the Nazis' lust for power, military aggressions, brutality, and inhumanity, he stated:

No charity can disguise the fact that the forces which these defendants represent, the forces that would advantage and delight in their acquittal, are the darkest and most sinister forces in society—dictatorship and oppression, malevolence [evil] and passion, militarism and lawlessness. By their fruits we best know them. Their acts have bathed the world in blood and set civilization back a century. They have subjected their European neighbors to every outrage and torture, every spoliation [looting] and deprivation that insolence, cruelty, and greed could inflict. They have brought the German people to the lowest pitch of wretchedness, from which they can entertain no hope of early deliverance. They have stirred hatreds and incited domestic violence on every continent. These are the things that stand in the dock shoulder to shoulder with these prisoners.[14]

Bombing Civilians

In presenting their case against the defendants, the Allied prosecutors first attempted to show the court that the Nazi regime had committed illegal, criminal acts. Then Jackson and his colleagues sought to establish that each defendant was guilty of specific war crimes. Whether it had been the regime or particular individuals who had committed the crimes, the evidence the prosecution presented for those offenses was both horrifying and damning.

In charging Hermann Göring with war crimes, for instance, the prosecutors noted that he was the head of Nazi Germany's air force, the Luftwaffe, in the early years of the war. That alone made him guilty of countless murders because the German planes dropped bombs directly on population centers and civilian targets. This was a repeated Nazi military tactic throughout the war, the prosecution pointed out. Another high-placed Nazi military leader who sat with Göring in the Nuremberg dock, Alfred Jodl, had openly stated this policy during the conflict. "Terror attacks against English centers of population," he had said, "will paralyze the will of the people to resist."[15]

> "Terror attacks against English centers of population will paralyze the will of the people to resist."[15]
>
> —High-placed Nazi Alfred Jodl.

Furthermore, the prosecutors said about Göring, besides his military role in Nazi Germany, he was tasked with eliminating Jews from economic and political life. Evidence showed clearly that both before and during the war, he had ordered Jewish businesses and property to be destroyed or taken over. At one point he had suddenly realized that demolishing those shops and companies served only to hurt Germany's economy. So he told one of his officers, "I wish you had killed 200 Jews and not destroyed such valuable property."[16]

The Question of Slave Labor

Another serious charge leveled at Göring, along with Alfred Rosenberg and other top Nazis in the dock, was that they either used or supported the use of slave labor. In fact, the prosecution stated, the Nazis had organized and run one of history's biggest forced labor programs. More than 20 million German civilians, foreign civilians, prisoners of war, and concentration camp inmates had been forced to perform slave labor at some point during the conflict. Moreover,

Hermann Göring (center) and Rudolf Hess listen to testimony during their trial for war crimes.

Trying to Shift the Blame

In his summation, delivered at the close of the trial, American prosecutor Robert Jackson addressed, among other things, the way the defendants had tried to shift the blame from themselves to others. Typically those "others" were Nazi leaders like Hitler and Himmler, who were already dead and therefore could neither admit nor deny their crimes. As Jackson said, "No matter how hard we have pressed the defendants on the stand, they have never pointed the finger at a living man as guilty." But blaming everything on Hitler was a ploy that would not work, Jackson said. "Hitler did not carry all responsibility to the grave with him," he added, and "all the guilt is not wrapped in Himmler's shroud." Jackson went on to say that Hitler

was a mad messiah who started the war without cause and prolonged it without reason. If he could not rule he cared not what happened to Germany. . . . He continued to fight when he knew it could not be won, and continuance meant only ruin. . . .

Hitler ordered everyone else to fight to the last and then retreated into death by his own hand. But he left life as he lived it, a deceiver; he left [behind a false] report that he had died in battle. This was the man whom these defendants exalted [as] a Fuhrer. It was they who conspired to get him absolute authority over all of Germany. And in the end he and the system they created for him brought the ruin of them all.

Quoted in Douglas Linder, "The Nuremberg Trials: Summation for the Prosecution by Justice Robert Jackson," University of Missouri–Kansas City School of Law. http://law2 .umkc.edu.

between a third and half of the slaves had been women, sometimes together with their children.

It seemed almost unbelievable to Jackson and the other prosecutors that the Nazis had not even attempted to hide this grievous crime. Indeed, Hitler had created an actual government position called chief of slave labor recruitment. That job went to Fritz Sauckel, another one of the defendants sitting in the courtroom's dock.

When called to the stand for questioning, Sauckel admitted that he knew that using forced labor was wrong. Yet he fell back on the excuse that Hitler, known to his countrymen as the Führer, had ordered him to organize and exploit millions of such laborers. Sauckel added that he felt it was his duty to obey Germany's dictator. "Hundreds of thousands of German soldiers had suffered terribly from the cold," Sauckel told the prosecutor:

> Many divisions had lost their arms and supplies. The [Führer] explained to me that if the race with the enemy for new arms, new munitions and new dispositions of forces was not won now, the Soviets would be as far as the [English] Channel by the next winter. Appealing to my sense of duty and asking me to put into it all I could, he gave me the task of obtaining new foreign labour for employment in the German war economy.[17]

When the prosecutor asked the defendant if he had had any doubts that this work was against international law, Sauckel replied, "There could be no misgivings on my part that the [forced] employment of foreign workers was against International Law."[18]

"The Jews Must Be Eliminated"

The prosecution showed that the Nazi leaders had committed numerous other war crimes. Yet none were as shocking and shameful as the mass murders of Jews, Slavic peoples, war prisoners, handicapped people, and others. Especially in the case of the Jews, the prosecution contended, there had been a concerted effort to commit genocide. Prosecutor Robert Jackson had alluded to these large-scale killings in his opening statement, calling them "so calculated, so malignant, and so devastating that civilization cannot tolerate their being ignored because it cannot survive their being repeated."[19]

Over the course of months, the prosecution demonstrated that the evidence for the mass murders was absolutely overwhelming. First, captured German documents contained hundreds of orders, speeches, and comments given by Nazi leaders related to the eradica-

Robert Jackson (at podium) was the chief American prosecutor at the Nuremberg Trials.

tion of Jews and others. Typical was Hans Frank's remark, "The Jews must be eliminated. Whenever we catch one, it is his end."[20]

There was also the damning physical evidence. It included many gas chambers, ovens still containing human remains, and huge pits filled with thousands of corpses. In addition, hundreds of death camp guards admitted to seeing the mass killings and other atrocities. Some of these witnesses told of an instance in which a group of children was gassed. When supplies of the lethal Zyklon B gas unexpectedly ran out, they testified, SS officers ordered the rest of the children to be tossed alive into red-hot ovens.

> "The Jews must be eliminated. Whenever we catch one, it is his end."[20]
>
> —Hans Frank, governor of Nazi-held Poland.

As if this evidence was not enough, the Nazis had actually made films showing, with seeming pride, the process of killing hundreds of people at a time and either incinerating or burying their bodies. In one movie shown by prosecutors, Nazi guards forced dozens of naked women to lie down in a ditch, ordered them to smile for the camera, then raised their machine guns and sprayed the terrified victims with bullets.

Prosecutors further showed how Nazi leaders, often along with their wives, felt no remorse or dishonor for such inhumane actions. To the contrary, they seemed to revel in the viciousness and horror. In one case the wife of a death camp commandant fashioned the tanned, tattooed skin from dead victims into lamp shades for her living room. Meanwhile, her husband used the shrunken head of a victim as a paperweight on his desk.

Defense Phase and Verdicts

Having presented reams of undeniable evidence for the defendants' war crimes, the prosecution rested on March 6, 1946. Jackson and his colleagues did not expect even more proof for those offenses to come out during the ensuing defense phase of the trial. Yet it did, mainly during the defendants' attempts to shift the blame to others or to make themselves seem less guilty than others.

First, as the Allied prosecutors had anticipated, most of the defendants used the excuse that they were just following Hitler's orders.

Pleading ignorance was another common ploy. A number of these top Nazis went so far as to claim they had no idea Germany had any concentration camps during the conflict. Such assertions were easily refuted, however. When Nazi foreign minister Joachim von Ribbentrop made this claim, the prosecution brought out a large map. It

A Deep Sense of Guilt

Although most of the defendants at Nuremberg attempted to shift the blame for their crimes onto others, one of them did not. Hans Frank, governor of Nazi-held Poland, testified that he did not set out to do terrible things. Yet by becoming a willing participant in the Nazi war effort, he had to share responsibility for the crimes the Nazis committed. After learning that Hitler had killed himself, Frank stated, "I resolved to reveal that responsibility of mine to the world as clearly as possible." Later in his testimony, he said, "speaking from the very depths of my feelings," he was "possessed by a deep sense of guilt." Then one of the prosecutors asked him, "Did you ever participate in the annihilation of Jews?" Frank answered yes and said:

My conscience does not allow me to throw the responsibility solely on these minor people. I myself have never installed an extermination camp for Jews, or promoted the existence of such camps; but if Adolf Hitler personally has laid that dreadful responsibility on his people, then it is mine too, for we have fought against Jewry for years; and we have indulged in the most horrible utterances; my own diary bears witness against me. Therefore, it is no more than my duty to answer your question in this connection with "yes." A thousand years will pass and still this guilt of Germany will not have been erased.

Quoted in Douglas Linder, "The Nuremberg Trials: Testimony of Hans Frank." University of Missouri–Kansas City School of Law. http://law2.umkc.edu.

showed clearly that several concentration camps were situated within a few miles of one of his homes.

Particularly damning was the testimony of Rudolf Hoess (not to be confused with Rudolf Hess, Hitler's second in command), long-time commandant of the Auschwitz death camp. Hoess was not one of the defendants. Apparently, the defense counsels thought that calling him as a witness and having him take responsibility for these murders would shift the blame from the Nazi higher-ups who were sitting in the Nuremberg dock. But this strategy backfired. Hoess *did* admit to gassing or otherwise killing untold numbers of Jews and others at his camp. But since some of those top Nazis had given the orders that Hoess had carried out, his admissions only served to strengthen the prosecution's case against them.

There seemed no doubt to anyone, therefore, that most of the defendants were guilty. In fact, when the verdicts came in on October 1, 1946, only three of them were acquitted: director of German radio programming Hans Fritzsche; minister of economics before the war Hjalmar Schacht; and ambassador to Turkey Franz von Papen. The other eighteen defendants were found guilty on one or more of the four main charges. Eleven were condemned to death by hanging, three received life sentences, two got twenty-year sentences, one a fifteen-year sentence, and one a ten-year sentence.

These, of course, were only the higher-level Nazis in custody. More than 180 captured lower-level individuals charged with war crimes were scheduled to face a series of trials beginning on December 9, 1946. Thus, while the eleven men sentenced to death went to the gallows in mid-October, the judgment of Nazi war criminals at Nuremberg was far from over.

CHAPTER FOUR

Other Holocaust War Crimes Trials

When most people hear the words *Nuremberg Trials*, they think of the well-publicized proceedings that lasted from 1945 to 1946, in which Hitler's top lieutenants were brought to justice. Yet these constituted the trials of only the most senior Nazi officials. Numerous other court cases were heard in Germany between 1945 and 1949. These involved lower-level Nazis such as SS officers, concentration camp guards, judges, doctors, and businessmen.

The Trials at Lüneburg

The so-called Belsen trial was one of these smaller but no less important public airings of the Nazis' many misdeeds. It unfolded in a high school in Lüneburg, in north-central Germany, beginning on September 11, 1945. The trial's official name was the Trial of Josef Kramer and Forty-Four Others. This was because Kramer, who had served in several concentration camps, including Bergen-Belsen, and gained a reputation for extreme brutality, was the primary defendant. But most people referred to it more simply as the Belsen trial.

Of the "forty-four others" tried at Lüneburg, most were lesser-known SS officers who were also accused of committing crimes against humanity. It is significant that some of the accused were women. Although the SS was an all-male organization, Nazi women sometimes worked closely with SS officers and therefore were frequently as guilty of terrible crimes as were the men. In addition, a few of the defendants were *kapos*, prisoners who had collaborated with the Nazis in exchange for better treatment.

For committing mass murders and other heinous crimes, many of the Belsen trial's defendants were severely punished. On November 17, 1945, Kramer was found guilty of both war crimes and crimes against humanity and sentenced to death by hanging. Ten other accused Nazis received the same sentence. Another eighteen defendants were deemed guilty and given prison sentences of one to fifteen years. Another SS man found guilty got a life sentence. But he had already received a death sentence for a different crime in an earlier military trial, so he ended up going to the gallows with Kramer. Meanwhile, fourteen of those tried at Lüneburg were acquitted of the charges, and one defendant was too ill to complete the trial.

The Subsequent Nuremberg Trials

Much larger in scope than the Belsen trial was a group of twelve trials held in Nuremberg after the main trials concluded there in October 1946. In contrast to the main trials in that city, which had been overseen by all four Allied powers, the twelve new proceedings were conducted solely by the United States. The formal name for these twelve trials was the Trials of War Criminals before the Nuremberg Military Tribunals. But over time they came to be called the Subsequent Nuremberg Trials for short. They took place between December 6, 1946, and April 13, 1949. The principal purpose of the Subsequent Nuremberg Trials was to bring to justice close to two hundred mid-level Nazi military officers and civilians. All were charged with playing prominent roles in the Holocaust and/or mass murders, employing slave labor, and other offenses against humanity.

A few of these trials involved one defendant. In the Milch Trial, for example, Field Marshall Erhard Milch was accused of cruel treatment and/or murders of prisoners of war. Milch stubbornly maintained that he had done nothing wrong. Moreover, while on the witness stand during the trial, he boldly shouted at the judge, saying, "You may think, and you are perfectly entitled to, that all Germans are criminals. And then you must say you are justified in simply hanging the lot. In which case you had better make a start with me!"[21] Milch was found guilty and sentenced to life in prison, but that sentence was later reduced, and he was released in 1954.

Most of the twelve proceedings, by contrast, involved multiple defendants. In the so-called Judges Trial, for instance, the prosecution went after sixteen German judges charged with using their authority to commit war crimes. Similarly, in the Flick Trial, six rich Germans who had run coal mines, steel plants, and other industrial concerns during the war were accused of using slaves supplied to them by the military. Another similar case involving the use of slave labor by corrupt industrialists was the Krupp Trial.

Gruesome Medical Experiments

The first of the twelve trials, the Doctors' Trial, took place between December 9, 1946, and August 20, 1947. Twenty-three Nazi physicians were charged with illegal and at times horrific medical experiments on human subjects. Typical was the case of Nazi doctor Karl Gebhardt, who had worked in Ravensbrück women's concentration camp, about 56 miles (90 km) north of Berlin. The prosecution

A former prisoner exhibits the scars left by Nazi doctors who performed experiments on her. Such experiments were intended to gain knowledge that could aid injured German soldiers.

charged Gebhardt with doing experiments on prisoners in hopes of using the knowledge gained to help injured German soldiers. In fact, this was the primary motive for the vast majority of medical experiments carried out by the defendants in the Doctors' Trial.

Gebhardt's specific crimes included breaking prisoners' legs with hammers and other tools, without the use of painkillers, and then infecting them with various germs. The wounds were allowed to fester until gangrene set in. At that point, Gebhardt employed various drugs to try to treat the gangrenous infections and kept records of the ones that showed promise. In a no less gruesome experiment, he cut off prisoners' limbs (again, without administering painkillers) and tried to transplant them onto German soldiers who had lost arms and legs in battle.

Another Nazi doctor, Viktor Brach, was accused of looking for ways to keep physically and mentally disabled people from reproducing. These individuals were seen as "useless eaters" by the Nazis, as were blind and deaf people. Brach and several Nazi physicians initially dealt with the disabled by sterilizing them. As the war wore on, however, the policy changed to simply killing them, since that was less expensive than sterilizing and continuing to feed and house them. As another Nazi doctor matter-of-factly stated about mentally ill persons, "As a National Socialist [Nazi], these creatures naturally only present to me a burden upon the healthy body of our nation."[22]

> "As a National Socialist [Nazi], these creatures naturally only present to me a burden upon the healthy body of our nation."[22]
>
> —A Nazi doctor.

Other Nazi physicians brought to justice in the Doctors' Trial were accused of a range of appalling acts. One defendant had tested biological warfare agents, such as bubonic plague and smallpox, on concentration camp prisoners. Another had tried to determine how effective various vaccines were against typhus, smallpox, cholera, and other terrible diseases. In such cases the doctor first infected the "patients," more properly the victims, with those diseases. Many of the prisoners who suffered through these inhumane tests died.

At the conclusion of the Doctors' Trial, the American judges rendered their verdicts. Seven of the twenty-three defendants, including Gebhardt and Brach, were sentenced to death by hanging. The executions took place in June 1948. Five of the defendants were acquitted, and the other eleven received prison sentences ranging from ten years to life.

Punishing the Death Squads

Among the twelve proceedings making up the Subsequent Nuremberg Trials, one that attracted an unusual amount of press attention was the Einsatzgruppen Trial, held from September 29, 1947, until April 10, 1948. The reason for this notoriety may have been the particularly shocking nature of the crimes involved. The Einsatzgruppen were death squads that worked mostly in Nazi-controlled eastern Europe. Their members murdered Jews, Slavs, Gypsies, disabled persons, and other civilians in huge numbers. From 1941 to 1943 alone, they slaughtered more than 1 million people.

> "Into the prisoner-of-war camps went the Einsatz units, selecting men for extermination, denying them the right to live."[23]
>
> —American Nuremberg Trials prosecutor Benjamin B. Ferencz.

In his opening statement, the American prosecutor, Benjamin B. Ferencz, summarized the standard and monstrous methods used by these death squads:

> Einsatz units entering a town or city ordered all Jews to be registered. They were forced to wear the Star of David under threat of death. All were then assembled with their families to be "re-settled" under Nazi supervision. At the outskirts of each town was a ditch, where a squad of Einsatz men waited for their victims. Whole families were arrayed, kneeling or standing near the pit to face a deadly hail of [machine gun] fire. Into the prisoner-of-war camps went the Einsatz units, selecting men for extermination, denying them the right to live. Helpless civilians were conveniently labeled "partisans" or "partisan-sympathizers" and then executed. In the hospitals and asylums the Einsatzgruppen destroyed the ill and insane, for "useless eat-

The Cold-Blooded Nazi Mind-Set

The defendants in the Subsequent Nuremberg Trials were all accused of committing horrible crimes against humanity, including mass murder. The American prosecutors and judges in these cases repeatedly called attention to the murderous, inhumane attitude of the officers who ordered the killings and the soldiers and others who carried them out. Such attitudes were clearly part of the cold-blooded Nazi mind-set. Such twisted thinking was made clear in a speech made by Nazi leader Heinrich Himmler in October 1943. He told a group of German generals:

> When somebody comes to me and says, "I cannot dig the anti-tank ditch with women and children, it is inhuman, for it would kill them," then I have to say, "You are a murderer of your own blood because, if the antitank ditch is not dug, German soldiers will die, and they are the sons of German mothers. They are our own blood." That is what I want to instill into this SS and what I believe have instilled into them as one of the most sacred laws of the future. Our concern, our duty is our people and our blood. It is for them that we must provide and plan, work and fight, nothing else. We can be indifferent to everything else. I wish the SS to adopt this attitude to the problem of all foreign non-Germanic peoples, especially Russians. All else is vain, fraud against our own nation and an obstacle to the early winning of the war.

Quoted in Douglas Linder, "The Subsequent Nuremberg Trials: Opening Statement of the Prosecution in the Einsatzgruppen Trial," University of Missouri–Kansas City School of Law. http://law2.umkc.edu.

ers" could never serve the Third Reich. Then came the gas vans, vehicles which could receive living human beings and discharge corpses. Every Einsatzgruppe had its allotment of these carriages of death.[23]

Nazi death squads known as Einsatzgruppen typically herded their victims into or near a pit or ditch, as this photo depicts, then murdered them in a mass execution.

The largest single mass murder committed by the Einsatzgruppen took place on September 29 and 30, 1941, at Babi Yar, situated about 2 miles (3.2 km) northwest of Kiev in Ukraine. The Nazi killers herded the victims together and led them to an enormous pit surrounded by a barbed wire fence and hundreds of German soldiers. The death squads selected about forty people at a time. The victims had to walk along a path lined with soldiers holding large clubs, which were used to pummel those who attempted to flee.

When the victims came to the pit, they were told to remove their clothes and lie down directly atop the bodies of people who had been executed earlier. While some of the victims begged for their lives, members of the squads shot them in the back of the head. During the two days in which this unbelievable act of cruelty occurred, at least 33,770 of Kiev's Jews were killed. When it was at last over, bulldozers covered the bodies with sand.

At the close of the trial, the head judge summarized the immensity of the Einsatzgruppen's crimes against humanity. Then he said,

"We have here participation in a crime of such unprecedented brutality and of such inconceivable savagery that the mind rebels against its own thought image and the imagination staggers in the contemplation of a human degradation beyond the power of language to adequately portray."[24] The court found all of the defendants guilty. Fourteen received death sentences, and two others were sent to prison for life. The rest got prison terms of varying lengths, but later, in the 1950s, most of these sentences were reduced.

Death in a Schoolhouse Cellar

Another of the US-sponsored Nuremberg Trials—the Pohl Trial—also generated a lot of interest in the press. The accused war criminal after whom the trial was named, Oswald Pohl, had joined the Nazi Party in 1926 and the SS in 1933. SS chief Heinrich Himmler had taken an interest in Pohl and became a sort of mentor to him, so the younger man rose quickly through the SS ranks.

The American prosecutors maintained that Pohl oversaw the organization of the Nazi concentration camps. This included distributing a set number of prisoners to each camp, as well as assigning certain groups of inmates to the military or German industry to be used for slave labor. Whether the prisoners were forced to work in the camps or in factories or elsewhere, they illustrated the Nazi theory that unwanted people could be eradicated through relentless forced labor. That is, they could be worked to death.

The prosecution held that Pohl was also involved in secret experiments held in the Neuegamme concentration camp, near the northern German city of Hamburg. There both adults and children were purposely infected with the debilitating disease tuberculosis. Once the victims were visibly sick, a Nazi doctor surgically removed their lymph nodes from their armpits and the harvested organs were sent to a hospital for study.

These acts were bad enough, prosecutors pointed out. But even worse was what happened in early 1945 when the Nazis realized that British troops were closing in on the Hamburg region. Pohl's superiors in Berlin ordered him to make sure that anything and any*one* involved in the experiments was eliminated before the British arrived.

Following this order, the American prosecutors said, Pohl gathered the twenty Jewish children, their four Jewish caretakers, and six Russian soldiers—all of whom had been subjected to the TB experiments. A truck carried them to an empty schoolhouse outside Hamburg. The Nazi guards then led the group to the building's cellar and injected them with a powerful drug to make them more pliable. Then they placed nooses around the prisoners' necks and hung them from big hooks protruding from a wall.

The Pohl Trial lasted from April 8 until November 3, 1947. In the end Pohl and three of his accomplices were found guilty of war

Oswald Pohl (in suit) at his trial in 1947. Found guilty of war crimes involving working prisoners to death and subjecting them to gruesome medical experiments, Pohl was sentenced to death by hanging.

crimes and sentenced to death by hanging. Some others who had taken part in those crimes were given prison sentences of between ten years and life, and three other accused individuals were acquitted.

Germany's "Supreme Law-Lord"

Unlike the culprits sentenced in the Einsatzgruppen and Pohl trials, the defendants in the Judges Trial (or Justice Trial) had what might be called "indirect" blood on their hands. That is, judges in courts across Nazi Germany had rendered biased verdicts. They had knowingly found certain people guilty only because they were Jewish, gay, or a member of some other group that Hitler deemed inferior. These judges were able to discriminate this way by taking advantage of several racial purity laws the Nazis had passed after coming to power. According to these statutes, members of "impure" groups of people were essentially guilty of the crime of simply being themselves.

The Judges Trial took place from March 5 to December 4, 1947. Sixteen former Nazi judges were charged with war crimes for sentencing numerous people to imprisonment or death without due cause. Not surprisingly, the defendants and their lawyers saw the charges very differently. They contended that the judges had no other choice but to follow the laws on the books. It was therefore the fault of those who had made the laws. The defense also pointed out that Hitler was the final judge in Nazi Germany. If a court judge had handed down a decision that Hitler disagreed with, Hitler would have both overturned the decision and had that judge killed.

The defendants brought up some of Hitler's specific statements about his supreme legal powers. "I do expect one thing," Hitler had said shortly before the war, "that the nation gives me the right to intervene" in court cases. In the future, he went on, he would "remove from office those judges who evidently do not understand the demand of the hour." In a later speech, moreover, Hitler had declared, "I am responsible for the fate of the German nation and hence [I am] the supreme law-lord of the German people."[25]

> "I am responsible for the fate of the German nation and hence [I am] the supreme law-lord of the German people."[25]
>
> —Nazi leader Adolf Hitler.

Dealing with "Useless Eaters"

Hitler and his Nazis used the derogatory term *useless eaters* to describe physically and mentally disabled people, blind and deaf people, and sufferers of epilepsy and similar disorders. At first, the Nazis looked for ways to keep such individuals from reproducing. Over time, however, they instituted a policy of exterminating them. This inhumane approach originated with two German university professors, Karl Binding and Alfred Hoche. Referring to the disabled, blind, and so forth in a book published in the 1930s, the two academics stated, "Their life is absolutely pointless." Moreover, "they are a terrible, heavy burden upon their relatives and society as a whole. Their death would not create even the smallest gap—except perhaps in the feelings of their mothers or loyal nurses."

Binding and Hoche also calculated society's total cost of caring for such people. It amounted, the two said, to "massive" amounts of "foodstuffs, clothing, and heating." Furthermore, their argument went, that cost was constantly draining the country's finances "for entirely unproductive purposes."

The exact number of disabled, blind, deaf, and other people of diminished capacity whom the Nazis exterminated during the war is unknown. But modern experts estimate it was more than seventy thousand. Back in the 1940s, one Nazi who agreed with Binding and Hoche's approach estimated that eliminating the "useless eaters" had saved Nazi Germany 885,439,980 Reich marks, roughly equivalent to $354 million in US currency during that era.

Quoted in Michael Burleigh, *Death and Deliverance: Euthanasia in Germany, c. 1900 to 1945*. Cambridge: University of Cambridge Press, 1994, pp. 17, 19.

The American prosecutors and judges did not accept this defense. They found ten of the sixteen defendants guilty of committing war crimes. They had shamefully "sold" their intellect and honor to Hitler, the court stated, in exchange for some temporary political authority and "the vain hope of personal security." Further, the court said, the judges had engaged in "the prostitution of a judicial system for the accomplishment of criminal ends."[26]

Of the ten Nazi judges found guilty, four received life sentences, and the others got shorter prison sentences. Four of the sixteen were acquitted. (One judge died during the trial, and another was too ill to take part.)

Hoping for Closure

Looking at all twelve of the Subsequent Nuremberg Trials together, 142 of the 185 defendants were convicted of crimes charged. Of those, 24 were sentenced to death, 20 got life in prison, and 98 were given shorter sentences. In addition, 35 defendants were acquitted. Four of the accused were too sick to complete their trials, and another 4 took their own lives during the proceedings.

The prosecutors, along with the public in the Allied countries, were satisfied that a measure of justice had been served. Yet one nagging thought continued to bother many people. It was that some Nazis who should have been tried at Nuremberg were still free. For the surviving victims and the families of those who had died, the thought of closure would not be possible until all those who had committed crimes were brought to justice.

CHAPTER FIVE

The Pursuit of Justice

By 1949, when the Subsequent Nuremberg Trials finished their work, most of the Nazi war criminals in custody had been tried and sentenced. Yet it was clear to Allied leaders, prosecutors, and judges that hundreds, and more likely thousands, of Nazi wrongdoers had fled in 1945. They were still at large and living in faraway lands. In the decades that followed, however, some of those war criminals were hunted down, caught, and tried. Others died before they could be found and brought to justice. And a few might still be alive and free, although they would have to be at least in their nineties and nearing the end of life.

Stangl Faces Justice

Typical of the cases in which Nazi perpetrators were hunted down and seized was that of Franz Stangl, one of the brutal commandants of the Treblinka concentration camp. For years he had enjoyed a comfortable life in Brazil. In 1967, however, famed Nazi hunter Simon Wiesenthal tracked him down. This quest began shortly after the end of the war. Wiesenthal had an associate keep a close watch on the house where Stangl's wife lived in the Austrian town of Bels. One day in 1949 some delivery men dropped off two large crates. One crate had the name *Damascus* printed on the outside. To Wiesenthal, this suggested that Stangl might be living in the Syrian city of Damascus. The problem was that there was no way to discover the former Nazi's specific address.

Matters rested that way until 1960, when Wiesenthal uncovered some clues that showed that Stangl had moved to South America, although exactly where in that continent was still a mystery. Four years later Wiesenthal found that his prey was hiding out in Brazil. Shortly after that, the Nazi hunter claimed, a former Gestapo guard visited him and said that he wanted to see Stangl suffer. "The big shots," the man said, "the Stangls, the Eichmanns. They got all the help when they needed it. They were smuggled overseas, they got money and jobs and forged papers. And who helps people like me? I have no work. I have no money!"[27] (Years later some reporters challenged this story, saying that that person who actually visited Wiesenthal was a disgruntled relative of Stangl's. But the Nazi hunter insisted this was not the case.) The man then gave Wiesenthal the address where Stangl lived in Brazil in exchange for $7,000. From there the West German authorities took over and extradited, or legally transferred, Stangl from Brazil to Germany. There the former camp commandant stood trial for his role in the murder of some nine hundred thousand people.

Smug and conceited, Stangl admitted that he had helped kill all those people. Yet he tried to defend his actions by shifting the blame. As so many other Nazis had done during the Nuremberg Trials, he claimed it was not his fault because he had merely followed orders in a warped system that Hitler had put in place. This was what Stangl told an interviewer who visited him in his German prison cell in 1970. She asked him if he could have stopped the brutal treatment of the inmates, but he said that was impossible because it was part of the complex and highly efficient system that Hitler had created. Indeed, he added, with a self-satisfied look on his face, "My conscience is clear. I was simply doing my duty!"[28]

> "My conscience is clear. I was simply doing my duty!"[28]
>
> —Treblinka commandant Franz Stangl.

Stangl received a sentence of life in prison. But he did not serve much of it, because he died of heart failure in his cell in 1971. Some observers argued that he had managed to cheat justice. Moreover, they said, the mere pursuit of justice was not enough to bring closure to the victims of the Nazi war criminals. Yet many others, including Wiesenthal, felt that justice *had* been served, mainly by finding Stangl, tearing him from his comfortable life, and making him endure a public airing of his crimes. "If I had done nothing else in my life but get this evil man," Wiesenthal stated, "I would not have lived in vain."[29]

An Aide to Ruthless Dictators

Another well-known case of a noted Nazi outlaw who was found and tried for his crimes was that of Klaus Barbie, widely known as the

"Butcher of Lyon." This unflattering nickname derived partly from the fact that he was the director of the Gestapo (Hitler's secret police) in the French city of Lyon during the Nazi occupation of France. Barbie not only tortured and killed many members of the French Resistance, he also sent thousands of Jews to the Auschwitz death camp, where they were starved, brutalized, and/or exterminated.

Like many other Nazi war criminals, Barbie fled to South America after the war. Settling in Bolivia, he changed his name to Klaus Altmann, and during the next forty or so years he befriended ruthless

Gestapo leader Klaus Barbie (center) escaped to Bolivia after World War II, but was arrested in 1983 and extradited to France, where he had committed most of his war crimes, for trial.

dictators and drug lords and engaged in various crimes. These included torturing and interrogating enemies of the dictatorships, advising the local secret police on how to find and deal with dissenters, and illegally obtaining weapons for the dictators.

"Where Are You Taking Me?"

By 1982, however, the political situation in Bolivia had changed significantly. A newly elected democratic president, Hernán Siles Suazo, was determined to ensure that democracy was firmly implanted in Bolivia. He also made it known that the ex-Nazi Barbie was no longer welcome in his country.

Toward that end, Suazo named popular journalist Gustavo Sanchez to lead a task force whose goal was to send Barbie back to France. Sanchez later recalled, "I was named deputy minister of the interior with one objective: to hand over Barbie to the French authorities within 24 hours."[30] French president François Mitterrand had secretly agreed that Barbie should be tried in France, since that was where the former Nazi had committed most of his war crimes. With that in mind, Sanchez's task force abruptly arrested Barbie for tax evasion. Not long afterward, Sanchez himself, accompanied by police officers, took Barbie to an airport, where a plane was waiting to take him to Lyon, France.

> "If I had done nothing else in my life but get this evil man, I would not have lived in vain."[29]
>
> —Nazi hunter Simon Wiesenthal.

Shortly before boarding the plane, Barbie asked, "Where are you taking me?" Sanchez answered that the destination was Lyon, to which the surprised Barbie exclaimed, "It cannot be." At that point, Sanchez later remembered,

> I said to him: "Yes, you are going back there. Do you remember the French adage which says that a criminal always returns to the scene of the crime? Don't you remember sending 600,000 Jews to concentration camps and gas chambers? As you personally killed so many in Lyon, you are going back there." "But," he said, "in war there are winners and losers." "So you lost," I said. "It is time to pay."[31]

In 1987 in Lyon, Barbie was tried and convicted of crimes against humanity. Because France had abolished the death penalty, he was sentenced to life in prison. Barbie served only a fraction of his sentence; he died in prison in 1991.

Finding Eichmann

The capture and trials of Stangl and Barbie made headlines around the world. But no other Nazi's ultimate appointment with justice was nearly as newsworthy as that of Adolf Eichmann, who had been Hitler's chief architect of the Holocaust. The story of his discovery and capture is a long and twisted one. Shortly after Eichmann's disappearance following the end of World War II, Simon Wiesenthal took advantage of an unusual coincidence. The Nazi hunter's landlady happened to know where Eichmann's parents lived, in the Austrian city of Linz. Wiesenthal told the German authorities, who questioned the parents, but they claimed they knew nothing about their son's whereabouts.

As time went on, Wiesenthal and others interested in tracking Eichmann down searched for clues to his location. A former Jewish refugee named Manus Diamant had some success when he secretly followed Eichmann's brother, then living in Germany, for months. This led him to Eichmann's wife and children, who were also still in Germany. In 1952, however, the wife and children disappeared, and Nazi hunters correctly gathered that they had left the country to join up somewhere with Eichmann. The reality was that they had reunited with him in Buenos Aries, Argentina.

Two separate investigations eventually confirmed that Eichmann was indeed in Argentina. First, Eichmann's father died in early 1960. Seeing this as an opportunity, Wiesenthal arranged for some private detectives to secretly photograph the mourners at the funeral. These photos became useful to Israel's intelligence service, Mossad. Its leaders also got wind of Eichmann's location in Argentina from Lothar Hermann, a half-Jewish German who had moved to that country in 1938. In 1960 Hermann's daughter Sylvia told him she was dating a young man named Klaus Eichmann, who had told her that his father had once been a Nazi. Hermann immediately told a lawyer he knew, who in turn told a friend who happened to be a Mossad agent.

Notorious Nazi leader Adolf Eichmann used this fake passport to enter Argentina, where he lived from 1950 until 1960, when he was captured and taken to Israel to stand trial.

With Hermann's permission, Mossad leaders asked Sylvia to go to her boyfriend's father's house to confirm that he was indeed Adolf Eichmann. When she knocked on the door, Eichmann himself appeared; she recognized him from wartime photos she had been shown.

Now knowing exactly where Eichmann resided, Israeli leaders decided to have Mossad capture him and take him to Jerusalem, where he would be tried as a war criminal. A team of Mossad agents snuck into Argentina and for several days observed the target's daily routine. They noted that he always rode a bus from his place of work (a local Mercedes-Benz factory) to his house at about the same time every afternoon. On May 11, 1960, they abducted him shortly after he had exited the bus. Then they smuggled him out Argentina and delivered him to the authorities in Israel.

"The Bottom Line"

In the decades that followed Eichmann's trial and execution in 1961, former Nazis who had escaped justice grew older and in many cases sicker or more frail. One after one, they passed away, although their

"A Beast, Not a Man"

The war crimes committed by Klaus Barbie came back to haunt him at his trial in Lyon, France, in 1987. Seven former residents of the city testified against the so-called Butcher of Lyon. They told how in 1944 he had tortured and murdered people, or ordered these actions to take place. Lise Lesevre, who had been a member of the French Resistance at the time, recalled being tortured on and off for almost three weeks. Barbie was looking for a Resistance leader named Didier and suspected that she knew who or where he was. Initially, she said, Barbie hung her up by the handcuffs that had been put on her wrists and then beat her with a rubber bar. "Who is Didier, where is Didier?" he kept repeating. When Lesevre refused to answer, Barbie put her in a bathtub containing freezing water. Repeatedly, he dunked her head under the water for long periods, but she never answered him. "During the bathtub torture," she told the prosecutor during the trial, "I wanted to drink to drown myself quickly. But I wasn't able to do it." When it was clear to Barbie that she was not going to talk, he threw her into a jail cell. "They would carry by the bodies of tortured people," she remembered. Barbie "was a beast, not a man. It was terror. He took pleasure in it."

Quoted in Literature of the Holocaust, "Klaus Barbie: Women Testify of Torture at His Hands," August 6, 2004. www.writing.upenn.edu.

names and whereabouts were often initially unclear to local authorities and Nazi hunters. Today, more than seventy years after the end of World War II, it is widely believed that most of them are dead. As one modern researcher puts it, "In the 21st century, it's assumed that most of the top officials who evaded justice have died one way or another. After all, a man who was 35 in 1940 would be 103 years old by 2008"[32] and 110 years old by 2015.

Nevertheless, some experts think that at least a few Nazi war criminals might still be alive. One of those experts is Efraim Zuroff, the director of the Simon Wiesenthal Center. In 2002 he and his associates launched Operation Last Chance, an earnest effort to find and bring to justice as many Nazi war criminals as possible before they die of old age. Initially, the Wiesenthal Center offered a reward of $10,000 for information leading to the conviction of one of those criminals. A few years later, however, they more than doubled the amount to $25,000.

Like other Nazi hunters, Zuroff now acknowledges that top Nazi officials who perpetrated the Holocaust and other war crimes during World War II are already dead. So Operation Last Chance has become a quest to find lower-level former Nazis. These include guards, soldiers, and others who murdered or helped murder innocent people at the orders of their superiors. The number of those lower-level helpers "is quite large, at least hundreds if not thousands,"[33] Zuroff argues. In fact, he says, it was not only Germans and Austrians who aided the Nazis during the conflict. Numerous citizens of other European nations helped the Nazis capture Jews and others who were eventually killed during the Holocaust.

> "The passage of time in no way diminishes the guilt of the perpetrator. If we were to set a chronological limit on prosecution, we would be saying that you could get away with genocide."[34]
>
> —Efraim Zuroff, director of the Simon Wiesenthal Center.

Zuroff adds that sometimes people ask him why he bothers to go after very elderly individuals who are no longer a threat to society. He answers:

> The passage of time in no way diminishes the guilt of the perpetrator. If we were to set a chronological limit on prosecution, we would be saying that you could get away with genocide, which is morally outrageous. We owe it to the victims to hold the perpetrators accountable. If someone murdered your grandmother and the murderer is only found 50 years later, it wouldn't very much concern you if this person was now elderly. You'd want him or her punished for the obvious reason that they murdered your grandmother. Every one of those victims was someone's grandmother or grandfather, son or daughter, and that's the bottom line.[34]

Aging War Criminals

Indeed, just such a case of arresting a now elderly low-level Nazi war criminal occurred in 1997. In September of that year, seventy-six-year-old Antony Sawoniuk, a retired British rail ticket inspector living in London, was arrested. Based on various tips from officials and witnesses in Russia and elsewhere, it became clear that he had been a Ukrainian policeman during World War II. Like many European policemen in Nazi-occupied countries, he had become a henchman for the Nazis.

Two witnesses to Sawoniuk's crimes were still living in the late 1990s. In the 1999 trial, one of them testified that he saw the defendant murder five Jews—three women and two men—in 1942. One of the women, the witness recalled, "did not want to take off her underpants. She was 28 or 29. When she refused, he threatened her with a truncheon [club]. When she had undressed, they were lined up and shot. He shot them with his pistol in the back of the head. He was standing behind each of them and levered them into the pit by raising his knee."[35]

The second witness against Sawoniuk told the court that he had watched the defendant line up fifteen women along the edges of a deep pit located near Poland's border with Belarus. Sawoniuk then mercilessly mowed them all down with a machine gun. For these crimes, the accused was convicted of multiple murders and sentenced to two life terms in prison. He died behind bars in 2005.

"We Must Be Vigilant"

Meanwhile, former Nazi Michael Karkoc, recently discovered living in Minnesota, is also in his nineties. He awaits trial on allegations that he played a major role in the horrifying massacre that took place in the Polish village of Chlaniow in 1944. If his case goes to trial, it could very well be one of the last such trials from the Holocaust.

The Allied leaders, prosecutors, and judges who tried the top Nazis at Nuremberg in the 1940s could never have foreseen that Nazi war criminals like Karkoc would still be hunted down and tried seventy years later. Moreover, those authorities could not imagine that genocide would be repeated in the world following the dismantling of the Nazi war machine and government. Thinking that such horrors were firmly in the past, one of the judges at Nuremberg stated that people everywhere could now "cherish the hope that civilization will actually redeem itself" and reaffirm "the holiness of life," trusting that "nothing even faintly resembling such a thing may happen again."[36]

A stack of skulls bears testimony to the mass murders that took place in the Asian country of Cambodia in the 1970s, providing a grisly reminder that genocide did not end with the Holocaust.

Rauff Denies Direct Involvement

To their regret, Nazi hunters were unable to return some of the most wanted war criminals to Germany to undergo trials. Among them was Walter Rauff, the SS officer who invented the gas vans that Nazi death squads employed to kill untold numbers of victims. Some idea of what his testimony might have been had he actually been tried appeared in 1972. In that year, Rauff volunteered to make a statement in a court case brought against another SS officer, Bruno Streckenbach. Rauff made the statement in Germany's embassy in Santiago de Chile. When the prosecutor cross-examined him and asked him about his own role in the Nazi mass killings, not surprisingly he denied any direct involvement, saying in part:

Regarding the annihilation of Jews in Russia, I know that gas vans were used for this purpose. I cannot say, however, when and to what extent this happened. . . . I know that at some time after my return [from naval service, I] learned that the gas vans were used for the execution of [death] sentences and for the killing of Jews. [As for] whether at that time I had doubts against the use of gas vans I cannot say. The main issue for me at the time was that the shootings were a considerable burden for the men who were in charge thereof and that this burden was taken off them through the use of the gas vans.

Quoted in Nizkor Project, "The Deposition of Walter Rauff," March 22, 2002. www.nizkor.org.

Yet in the decades that followed Nazi Germany's defeat, such crimes against humanity happened again. In Cambodia in the 1970s and Rwanda and the former Yugoslavia in the 1990s, millions more innocents fell prey to the horrors of genocide. Eventually, it became clear that the potential for the repetition of such horrors is, and likely will long be, present. In 2005, the sixtieth anniversary of the liberation of the Nazi death camps, United Nations secretary-general Kofi Annan addressed this issue of possible future genocides. He suggested that people might be able to stop such examples of inhumanity from happening by openly opposing the deep, irrational hatred that motivates them. If, for example, the Allies had found a way to neutralize Hitler and his twisted hatreds before he could start a world war, there might never have been any Nazi war criminals in the first place. In short, Annan stated, "We must be vigilant against all ideologies based on hatred and exclusion, whenever and wherever they may appear."[37]

SOURCE NOTES

Introduction: Time Is Their Enemy

1. Quoted in Associated Press, "A Leader of Nazi SS-Led Unit That Massacred Civilians, Michael Karkoc, Has Been in U.S. Since 1949," CBS News, June 14, 2013. www.cbsnews.com.
2. Quoted in Valery Hache, "Never Too Late: Nazi Hunters Tirelessly Pursue 50 Elderly Auschwitz War Criminals," NBC News, May 12, 2013. http://worldnews.nbcnews.com.

Chapter One: The Coward's Way Out

3. Quoted in Scrapbookpages.com, "Treblinka Death Camp," August 24, 2009. ww.scrapbookpages.com.
4. Quoted in Holocaust Website, "Sobibor: Franz Stangl." www.auschwitz.dk.
5. Quoted in Susannah Cahalan, "Rantings of a Nazi Monster," New York Post, February 27, 2010. http://nypost.com.
6. Quoted in William L. Shirer, The Rise and Fall of the Third Reich. New York: Simon and Schuster, 2011, p. 978.

Chapter Two: Former Nazis on the Run

7. Karl Dönitz, Memoirs: Ten Years and Twenty Days, trans. R.H. Stevens. Cleveland, OH: World, 1959, p. 449.
8. Quoted in Hilary Gaskin, Eyewitnesses at Nuremberg. London: Arms and Armour, 1991, pp. 25–26.
9. Quoted in Illustrated London News, "German Atrocities in Prison Camps," April 28, 1945, p. 459.
10. Quoted in David Cesarani, Eichmann: His Life and Crimes. London: Vintage, 2005, p. 321.

Chapter Three: The Nuremberg Trials

11. Hannah Arendt, Eichmann in Jerusalem: A Report of the Banality of Evil. New York: Penguin, 1977, p. 252.

12. Quoted in Douglas Linder, "The Nuremberg Trials," University of Missouri–Kansas City School of Law. http://law2.umkc.edu.

13. Quoted in Douglas Linder, "The Nuremberg Trials: Justice Jackson's Opening Statement for the Prosecution," University of Missouri–Kansas City School of Law. http://law2.umkc.edu.

14. Quoted in Linder, "The Nuremberg Trials: Justice Jackson's Opening Statement for the Prosecution."

15. Quoted in Douglas Linder, "The Nuremberg Trials: Defendants in the Major War Figures Trial," University of Missouri–Kansas City School of Law. http://law2.umkc.edu.

16. Quoted in Linder, "The Nuremberg Trials: Defendants in the Major War Figures Trial."

17. Nizkor Project, "The Trial of German Major War Criminals: Sitting at Nuremberg, Germany, Tuesday, May 28, 1946." www.nizkor.org.

18. Nizkor Project, "The Trial of German Major War Criminals."

19. Quoted in David Irving, *The Rise and Fall of the Luftwaffe: The Life of Field Marshall Erhard Milch*. New York: Little, Brown, 1973, p. 364.

20. Quoted in Michael Burleigh, *Death and Deliverance: Euthanasia in Germany, c. 1900 to 1945*. Cambridge, UK: University of Cambridge, 1994, p. 45.

Chapter Four: Other Holocaust War Crimes Trials

21. Quoted in Irving, *The Rise and Fall of the Luftwaffe*, p. 364.

22. Quoted in Burleigh, *Death and Deliverance*, p. 45.

23. Quoted in Douglas Linder, "The Subsequent Nuremberg Trials: Opening Statement of the Prosecution in the Einsatzgruppen Trial," University of Missouri–Kansas City School of Law. http://law2.umkc.edu.

24. Quoted in Douglas Linder, "The Subsequent Nuremberg Trials: Military Tribunal II, Case 9," University of Missouri–Kansas City School of Law. http://law2.umkc.edu.

25. Quoted in Douglas Linder, "The Subsequent Nuremberg Trials: The Justice Trial," University of Missouri–Kansas City School of Law. http://law2.umkc.edu.

26. Quoted in Linder, "The Subsequent Nuremberg Trials: The Justice Trial."

Chapter Five: The Pursuit of Justice

27. Quoted in Tom Segev, *Simon Wiesenthal: The Life and Legends*. New York: Doubleday, 2010, p. 208.
28. Quoted in Holocaust Website, "Sobibor."
29. Quoted in Guy Walters, *Hunting Evil: The Nazi War Criminals Who Escaped and the Quest to Bring Them to Justice*. New York: Random House, 2010, p. 337.
30. Quoted in *Guardian* (London), "In Pursuit of Bolivia's Secret Nazi," September 10, 2008. www.theguardian.com.
31. Quoted in *Guardian* (London), "In Pursuit of Bolivia's Secret Nazi."
32. Josh Clark, "Are There Nazi War Criminals Still Alive?," How StuffWorks. http://history.howstuffworks.com.
33. Quoted in David Crossland, "Operation Last Chance: Nazi Hunters More than Double Reward to $25,000," *Spiegel Online*, January 14, 2008. www.spiegel.de.
34. Quoted in Crossland, "Operation Last Chance."
35. Quoted in Walters, *Hunting Evil*, p. 405.
36. Quoted in Linder, "The Subsequent Nuremberg Trials: Military Tribunal II, Case 9."
37. Quoted in United Nations, "Such an Evil Must Never Be Allowed to Happen Again, Secretary-General Tells General Assembly Session Commemorating Liberation of Nazi Death Camps," press release, January 24, 2005. www.un.org.

IMPORTANT PEOPLE

Klaus Barbie

Widely known as the Butcher of Lyon, he murdered and tortured members of the French resistance as well as ordinary French citizens. After fleeing to Bolivia in 1945, he committed more atrocities there to help keep that country's brutal dictator in power.

Adolf Eichmann

One of the top Nazi perpetrators, he was in charge of organizing Hitler's Final Solution, the planned mass murder of all of Europe's Jews. Although he found refuge in South America after the war, in the early 1960s the Israeli secret police tracked him down and brought him to Israel, where he was tried and executed.

Kurt Franz

One of the commandants of the Treblinka concentration camp, at the end of the war he tried to evade capture by blending back into Germany's population. It worked for a while. But in 1959 he was caught, and later he was tried and received a life sentence.

Robert Jackson

A justice of the US Supreme Court, he was appointed by US president Harry Truman to the post of lead American prosecutor at the Nuremberg war crimes trials held from 1945 to 1946. Jackson delivered the long, eloquent opening statement on behalf of all the Allied prosecutors.

Michael Karkoc

Found living at age ninety-four in Minneapolis, Minnesota, in 2013, he was arrested for his leading role in a Nazi massacre of innocent villagers in Poland in 1944. In early 2015 he was still awaiting a trial.

Josef Mengele

The so-called Angel of Death, he was a Nazi doctor who performed unspeakable experiments on inmates at the infamous Auschwitz death camp. When the Allies defeated Nazi Germany, he fled to South America, where he died in the 1970s. The popular movie *The Boys from Brazil* presents a semifictional account of Mengele's post-war activities.

Eduard Roschmann

Called the Butcher of Riga, he was a Nazi officer who brutalized people in Latvia after that nation was conquered by Germany in the early years of World War II. With the Allies closing in during the conflict's final weeks, Roschmann fled Germany with the aid of Catholic churchmen who sympathized with the Nazis.

Franz Stangl

A leading Nazi officer at Treblinka and several other concentration camps, he helped gas hundreds of thousands of Jews and other supposed "inferiors." At the war's close, he fled to Brazil but was later caught and tried for his war crimes. Although he received a life sentence, he died after serving only a small part of it.

Simon Wiesenthal

The most famous of the post–World War II Nazi hunters, he founded the Simon Wiesenthal Center, dedicated to bringing Nazi war criminals to justice. He was credited with tracking down numerous former Nazis, including Franz Stangl.

Efraim Zuroff

Director of the Simon Wiesenthal Center office in Jerusalem, he is an American Israeli historian and a dedicated Nazi hunter. In 2002 Zuroff helped launch Operation Last Chance, a last-ditch effort to track down and punish former Nazi criminals before they die.

FOR FURTHER RESEARCH

Books

Neal Bascomb, *Hunting Evil: How a Band of Survivors and a Young Spy Agency Chased Down the World's Most Notorious Nazi*. Boston: Houghton Mifflin, 2009.

Neal Bascomb, *The Nazi Hunters*. New York: Levine, 2013.

David Cesarani, *Eichmann: His Life and Crimes*. Boston: Da Kapo, 2007.

Saul Friedlander, *Nazi Germany and the Jews: The Years of Extermination, 1939–1945*. New York: HarperCollins, 2008.

Eva M. Kor and Lisa R. Buccieri, *Surviving the Angel of Death: The True Story of a Mengele Twin in Auschwitz*. Terre Haute, IN: Tanglewood, 2012.

Paul Roland, *The Nuremberg Trials: The Nazis and Their Crimes Against Humanity*. London: Arcturus, 2012.

William L. Shirer, *The Rise and Fall of the Third Reich*. New York: Simon and Schuster, 2011.

Gerald Steinacher, *Nazis on the Run: How Hitler's Henchmen Fled Justice*. New York: Oxford University Press, 2011.

Nikolaus Wachsmann and Jane Caplan, eds., *Concentration Camps in Nazi Germany: The New Histories*. London: Routledge, 2010.

Guy Walters, *Hunting Evil: The Nazi War Criminals Who Escaped and the Quest to Bring Them to Justice*. New York: Random House, 2010.

Internet Sources

Gerald L. Posner and John Ware, "Fugitive: How Nazi War Criminal Josef Mengele Cheated Justice for 34 Years," *Chicago Tribune*, May 18, 1986. http://articles.chicagotribune.com/1986-05-18/features/8602040597_1_josef-mengele-field-hospital-red-army.

Simon Wiesenthal Archive, "Franz Stangl." www.simon-wiesenthal
-archiv.at/02_dokuzentrum/02_faelle/e02_stangl.html.

YouTube, "The Eichmann Trial." www.youtube.com/user/Eichmann
TrialEN.

Websites

Holocaust, Jewish Virtual Library (www.jewishvirtuallibrary.org/j
source/holo.html). An excellent resource for information about the
Holocaust, with dozens of links leading to articles about all aspects of
that terrible event.

**Nuremberg Trials: Brief Overview of Defendants and Verdicts,
Jewish Virtual Library** (www.jewishvirtuallibrary.org/jsource/Holo
caust/verdicts.html). This useful site provides information about the
crimes, charges, and sentences of the principal Nazis in these famous
legal proceedings.

**Sentencing and Execution of Nazi War Criminals, 1946, Eye-
Witness to History.com** (www.eyewitnesstohistory.com/nuremberg
.htm). Dr. G.M. Gilbert, an American prison psychologist during
the Nuremberg Trials, recalls some of the conversations he had with
leading Nazis accused of war crimes.

Simon Wiesenthal Center (www.wiesenthal.com). The main website
of Simon Wiesenthal's important organization, dedicated to finding
Nazi war criminals and raising awareness of the Holocaust.

**Uncovering the Architect of the Holocaust: The CIA Names File
on Adolf Eichmann, National Security Archive** (www2.gwu.edu
/~nsarchiv/NSAEBB/NSAEBB150/index.htm). The leading American intelligence agency, the CIA, presents this authentic declassified
collection of documents related to the hunt for and capture of Nazi
war criminal Adolf Eichmann.

US Holocaust Memorial Museum (www.ushmm.org). The museum's website provides many links to articles about Nazi war crimes,
anti-Semitism, and lectures with titles such as "Just Following Orders? How Ordinary People Become Perpetrators."

INDEX

Note: Boldface page numbers indicate illustrations.

PICTURE CREDITS